SHINE ON MAYBERRY MOON

Aaron McAlexander

Published by Stonebridge Press

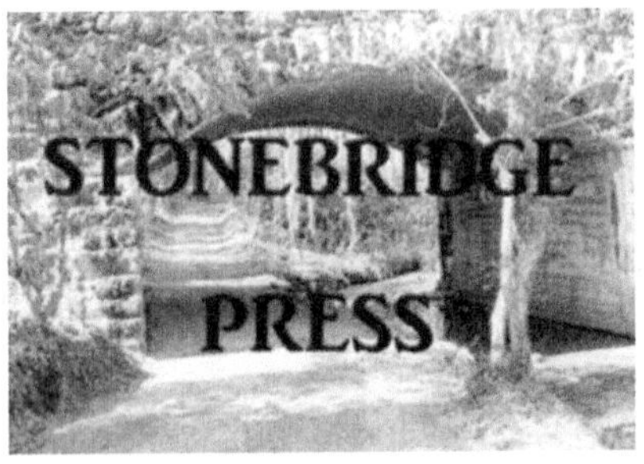

ISBN-13: 978-1977608017

Printed in U.S.A.

Third Printing

CONTENTS

PROLOGUE

From the time humans first discovered that it is possible to get a buzz from eating fermented grapes, they appear to have been searching for more and better ways to create drinkable forms of alcohol. There is archeological evidence that humans have been imbibing for such a long time that they may have learned how to brew beer before they knew how to bake bread. There is evidence that wine was being consumed in China as early as 7000 BC, and evidence that it was being made and consumed in Persia and Mesopotamia by 4500 BC. Biblical history indicates that the ritual consumption of wine was a Jewish practice dating back to about the same period.

The oldest commercial winery archaeologists have yet to discover was recently found in Armenia. There they found an ancient establishment located in a cave, complete with a grape press, storage jars, drinking cups, just sitting there waiting for customers since 4100 BC. The earliest evidence for the production and consumption of beer was found in Iran and it dates from around 5000 BC. Ancient hieroglyphs tell us that beer was a part of the daily diet of the Egyptian Pharaohs back in about the same period.

Historians hypothesize that the desire to cultivate grain for the purpose of making beer is one reason early cultures abandoned life as nomadic hunter-gatherers and formed permanent agricultural communes. It is ironic that most of the earliest evidence of human consumption of wine and beer has been found in parts of the world where the population largely became Islamic and the consumption of alcohol came to be prohibited. The prohibition of alcohol in the Middle East does not appear to have created a region populated by peaceful and stable societies, however.

Although legend has it that Saint Patrick, who some claim to have originally been from Scotland, introduced distilling into Ireland in the Fifth Century A.D., the earliest direct evidence of the distillation of alcohol comes from southern Italy and dates back to the early 12th century. It is not surprising to learn that Irish whiskey and German schnapps both began to be produced shortly thereafter.

The significance of the distillation process is the resulting concentration of the alcohol. In an undistilled beverage such as beer or wine, the fermenting yeast is killed off when the alcohol reaches a concentration of about ten to fifteen percent. In the distillation process, the alcohol is evaporated from beer or wine and collected in concentrations ranging from about 30 to 60 percent. The vapor boiled off in the process was once called "spirit" and that is why distilled forms of alcoholic beverages continue to be called "spirits." In America, the term "hard liquor" has been a term commonly used to distinguish distilled spirits from lower alcohol content beverages such as beer and wine since colonial times.

Much of the production of the moonshine that is so closely associated with the Southern Appalachian Region of the United States can be attributed to the knowledge and tradition of making distilled spirits that was brought in by the Scots Irish who settled there in the late eighteenth and early nineteenth centuries.

The record of alcohol distillation in Scotland goes back into the fifteenth century, and of course, the Scottish Parliament began taxing spirits soon thereafter. Following the Act of Union with England in 1707, taxes on distilled spirits became so onerous that the Scottish distilling business was driven underground. Records indicate that by the early 1800's, hundreds of illicit stills were being confiscated in Scotland every year, but those confiscations apparently had little effect on the amount of duty-free whisky being produced and consumed by the Scots.

Most of the Scots who immigrated to America from Northern Ireland originally settled in Pennsylvania, but following the enforcement of the whisky tax in 1792, and the resulting Whisky Rebellion, many of the people affected moved down the Appalachians into Virginia, Kentucky, Tennessee, and North Carolina. Those Scotsmen brought their skill in constructing small pot stills and their tradition of conducting covert distillation operations with them, and the rest, as they say, is history.

It is has been well documented that at the time of his death in 1799, George Washington was one of the largest whisky producers in the newly formed United States. Legend also has it that he was originally opposed to the idea of operating a distillery, but that he was talked into it by his Scottish plantation manager, James Anderson. The whisky he made had a lot more in common with traditional moonshine than with what most people think of as whisky today. Although it was mostly made from rye rather than corn, it was sold as unaged "white" liquor, just like most of the white corn liquor made in America for the next century. "Red" liquor, such as American Bourbon or imported Scotch

Whisky did not gain popularity in America until near the end of the nineteenth century.

The famous Southern Appalachian moonshine was originally white corn liquor, but the ingredients used evolved somewhat over the last hundred years. When corn liquor was first being made in America, refined cane sugar was extremely expensive and seldom used in liquor at all. To make the most basic form of corn liquor, first the corn had to be allowed to sprout, then it was ground, and then allowed to ferment from naturally occurring wild yeasts. The fermentation could sometimes be assisted by the addition of a little horse manure. If malted barley could be obtained, combining it with the sprouted corn both aided in the fermentation and produced a smoother tasting liquor.

Later, when malt and baker's yeast became available, cracked corn or corn meal, rather than sprouted corn, was increasingly used to make moonshine. On into the twentieth century, as refined cane sugar became relatively less expensive, it eventually became the dominant ingredient used in the making of moonshine. During both of the World Wars, the scarcity of key ingredients such as sugar created an increasing reliance on innovative recipes that often included various forms of commercial livestock feed. Also, as moonshining became larger in scale and the product was more and more being made to sell rather than drunk by the distillers themselves, the chance of getting liquor that had been adulterated with a chemical such as lye or embalming fluid increased dramatically.

Over the past century, the most widely used main ingredient used in the making of moonshine has evolved from being sprouted corn, through formulations that tended to use less corn and more sugar. If the recipes one can now read on the internet are true indications of how moonshine is being made today, it is mostly being made from sugar, water, malt, yeast, and just possibly just a little corn in one form or another.

One question I often hear asked is whether the alcohol found in alcoholic beverages is *ethanol*, the same kind of alcohol that is currently being added to gasoline in the United States. The answer is a definitive *yes*. The very same kind of alcohol currently found in concentrations of up to 10 percent in our gasoline, and which some people blame for gumming up the fuel systems of their pickups and making their chainsaws hard to start, is also sold in liquor stores. There it can be found, often packaged in *plastic* bottles, and available in concentrations of 40 to 50 percent, and labeled as vodka or gin or any of a plethora of other spirits.

The subject of "kinds of alcohol" having been broached, perhaps a brief chemistry lesson is in order. This book is not intended to be a science text, so if you think a few chemical details related to alcohol will be just too boring to read, I recommend that you flip on over to the next chapter. But as anyone familiar with moonshine knows, there several ways that toxic forms of alcohol can get into the drinkable stuff that reliable moonshiners try to produce. The following is just some information that might help people who are interested in making (or even just sampling) a little moonshine be sure that it is safe.

In chemistry, the name *alcohol* applies to any organic compound in which there is a hydrogen-oxygen ion bound to a carbon atom or chain of carbon atoms. (The oxygen-hydrogen combination is frequently written using the symbol OH.) The simplest of the alcohols has a single carbon atom and is represented in the form of a chemical formula as CH_3OH. This alcohol is known as either *methanol* or *methyl alcohol*, and it is also often called wood alcohol. The next simplest alcohol has two carbon atoms and is represented in chemical symbolism as C_2H_5OH. This alcohol is known as *ethanol* or *ethyl alcohol*, and sometimes called grain alcohol. The next most complex alcohol has three carbon atoms, and you are probably getting the picture. That alcohol is C_3H_7OH or *isopropyl alcohol,* and is often called rubbing alcohol. The list of alcohols goes on and on, with the next example being C_4H_9OH or *butyl alcohol*, and so forth.

When the term *alcohol* is used in the context of something that is intended to be drunk, that alcohol is most assuredly ethyl alcohol. Ethyl alcohol (ethanol) is the only alcohol that can be taken internally in any significant quantity without severe consequences, and there are many people who would even disagree with that.

The alcohol most often used as a germicide is usually called denatured alcohol because it is most often simply ethanol that contains additives intended to make it poisonous, bad tasting, foul smelling, or all of those things. Methanol can be added to “denature" ethanol, thereby making it poisonous, or the addition of a chemical called pyridine will make it foul smelling. Sometimes, a chemical called denatonium benzoate, the bitterest substance on earth, is added. In the United States, making the alcohol unfit for human consumption frees the manufacturer from the requirement of paying federal excise taxes on it.

Just like it says on the label, the ingestion of even a

small quantity of denatured alcohol can result in severe gastric distress, blindness, and even death. There is really no simple way in which most denaturing agents can be separated from denatured ethanol. Unfortunately, during the prohibition years in the United States, misleading myths such as the claim that denaturing agents could be removed by straining alcohol through a loaf of bread resulted in the deaths of several hundred people a year.

One of the major hazards that has been associated with moonshine since its earliest beginnings is the contamination of the ethanol with some toxic form of alcohol such as methanol, and it usually gets into the moonshine in one of two ways. First, all but the most precise distillation of fermented grains and fruits will also release a small percentage of methanol. Methanol evaporates at a lower temperature than ethanol, so if the first ten or fifteen percent of a first run is caught and discarded, and the distillation process is ended after distilling off the ethanol and before the temperature is allowed to go too high, methanol contamination will mostly be eliminated. Another way methanol sometimes gets into the hooch is when unscrupulous moonshiners add industrial solvents as "stretchers" to increase the kick and volume of the product. As stated earlier, lye is sometimes also used for the same purpose.

Although it is well known that the production of safe and acceptable quality moonshine is highly dependent upon controlling the temperature during the distillation process, I have yet to see a picture of a vintage Appalachian still that has a thermometer sticking out of the boiler.

The claim is sometimes made that the presence of contaminants in alcohol can be revealed by the color of the flame when it is burned, but that is generally an unreliable test. It is true that if a sample of alcohol burns with a red flame, it may contain lead, but since ethanol burns with a blue flame and methanol burns with an invisible flame, igniting a sample of hooch is not likely to reveal if it there is any methanol present.

Assembling this collection of stories about people I have known and their experiences related to moonshine liquor has been something of a stretch for me, given that I have never made nor hauled any. In fact, the few times that I have ever actually drunk any, it usually has been in the interest of research related to my writing. Honest. It is true that I have known a few people who made moonshine and a few others who transported it, and I have listened to many interesting stories told by former drinkers, makers, and haulers. I also have a good friend who was a chemist and whose family was seriously involved in the moonshining business a couple of generations ago. There is a lot of interesting information in this book that he provided, but he insists that he remain anonymous.

As a kid growing up in these Blue Ridge Mountains, some of the adult conversations I would hear caused me to think that perhaps Mayberry was inhabited by two just kinds of people, folks who were either teetotalers or drunks. When I got a little older and began to do some observing on my own, I found there was a third group of people living in the area. I discovered that there were some folks who maintained a public appearance of total abstinence, but who would sometimes take a quick snort if there was booze available and the chance of their being observed was sufficiently small.

There really were plenty of reasons for folks to be concerned about the consumption of alcohol in the time and place where I was growing up, but I do think that some of the teetotalers I knew carried their campaign against alcohol a little to the extreme. I'll give just one example.

When I was a kid in elementary school, we would have a short period each morning during which the class would sing a couple of songs before the studies began. A parent from the community complained to the principal because our class would sometimes sing the traditional African-American ballad, *Jimmy Crack Corn*. The parent's objection was based on just one line in the first verse of the song, the verse that goes…

"When I was young I used to wait
On Massa and give him his plate,
And pass the bottle when he got dry
And brush away the blue tail fly."

It seems that the parent had a problem with the "pass the bottle" line. Now, nowhere does the song say what was in the bottle passed to Ol' Massa, but given the possibility that it may have contained alcohol, the parent thought the verse should either be skipped or the wording changed; whatever was required to eliminate any possibility of the song having a negative influence on the minds of the little children. I think it is unlikely that even one kid singing that song in our classroom had ever given a thought about what might have been in the bottle being passed, at least until the parent brought up the subject. (Note: The late TV kiddie cowboy Fred Kirby used to substitute "Pet Milk" for "bottle" in the song, but I suspect that was a case of product placement for his sponsor.)

I can't imagine what would have happened if we had dared to sing *That Good Ole Mountain Dew* during song time at school. Most of the kids I knew could sing every verse of that song, but I think they were all aware that the verses were mostly tongue-in-cheek.

The people I have known or known about who actually drank the "stuff" – moonshine, 'shine, mountain dew, white lightning, hooch, booze – whatever the name of choice, appeared to drink it for one or more of a few basic reasons. While I do think that moonshine was often consumed as an act of defiance against authority and sometimes drunk as a perceived display of manliness, it was most often imbibed because of the desire to soften the reality of the hard life in these mountains.

Moonshine was (and still is) sometimes consumed for its alleged medicinal properties, of course. But when you get right down to the basics, the preponderance of the moonshine consumed in these mountains was drunk simply because it was the only intoxicating beverage available for people who had a hankering for something alcoholic to drink. It may have been *aqua vitae* to some, but I can't ever recall hearing anyone claim that they drank moonshine just because it tasted so good.

Moonshine? In Mayberry?

Mama would be furious, rest her soul, and that would be for several reasons. She might not be all that angry just because her son is writing about moonshine, but she would certainly be upset about his not being unequivocally condemning of all alcoholic drink and decrying its very existence. A major concern would be the possibility that my writing might lead some people to believe that once upon a time, there were people who were making moonshine liquor in and around her beloved home community of *Mayberry,* Virginia. The part that would infuriate Mama the most, however, would be when I allege that some of those Mayberry residents who were involved in that nonexistent moonshining might have been kinfolk of ours. Not really close relatives, mind you, but close enough kin that their involvement in the business was a subject about which we were supposed to never utter a word. To this day, I can recall a brief conversation I had with Mama about something I had overheard at school.

"Mama, is it true that Uncle Leon and Cousin Grover are running a still? Do they really make moonshine likker?" I ventured.

"Harrumph! We don't talk about that in this family!" Mama put an end to that conversation in short order.

My mother was truly my grandmother's daughter, and my grandmother was the staunchest, the most dedicated, and the most unwavering enemy of alcohol – in all of its drinkable forms – I have ever known. Moonshine or Wild

Turkey, Glenmorangie or rotgut, Cabernet or scuppernong, anything drinkable that contained alcohol was nothing other than *demon rum,* so far as she was concerned.

Mama followed her own mother's example with just the tiniest bit of moderation. She would reluctantly admit that there possibly were a few people in this world who might take a drink that contained [a little] alcohol on [rare] occasions and not immediately become hopelessly addicted to the stuff. She might even admit that some of those people were never known to have deprived or abused their families. After making any such admission, however, Mama would be sure and add that the moderate drinkers one might read about in magazines or see on television were mostly city people from somewhere up North, and they were part of a culture that was very different than our own Southern Appalachian heritage. The social partaking of spirits by those people was just a part of their shallow pseudo-sophistication, she would declare, and if the truth be known, a lot of them did indeed become dependent on the stuff. She would also be likely to point out that even though there are some people who can drink alcohol and not become alcoholics, it still is advisable for anyone to avoid the risk by never taking the first drink. I was never able to argue with her logic on that point.

When Richard C. Davids' acclaimed book, *The Man who Moved a Mountain*, came out in the 1970's, there was quite a lot of criticism of the book bantered about in Mayberry. Much of the book is about events that occurred in Mayberry and nearby communities in the early twentieth century, and while it is understandable that the author may have gotten some of the family relationships a bit confused, it is also true that he made this region of the Blue Ridge

Mountains of Virginia appear more backward and violent than was actually the case. All of that was done in the process of creating an exciting and interesting book, of course, and I do think that the book does provide some insight into what life was like in the region at the time. Mama, who did not worry so much about the inaccuracies of the family histories, reserved most of her criticism for what she considered to be an unfair representation of the amount of illegal liquor made and consumed in Mayberry and the surrounding area during the period about which the book was written.

One example of Davids' hyperbole used in describing the people of the area is where he wrote that *most* families in the region had their own stills to provide their "daily usin' liquor," and that the family passed the bottle around the table every morning, even encouraging young children to have a dram "to help ward off disease." Mama and I had a conversation about what might have been Davids' definition of "most families," and I did agree with her that this description could have applied to only a very few families anywhere near Mayberry.

There have been other authors who wrote about the area and who made many references to the Mayberry denizens who practiced the art of making moonshine and the much larger number that drank a lot of it. Some of those stories were penned by Mama's own brother, John Hassell Yeatts, and they were especially irritating to her. John Hassell Yeatts was a writer who grew up in Mayberry, and a man who was also something of a connoisseur of spirits, fine and otherwise. When challenged by my mother regarding the extent of moonshining around Mayberry, he would start enumerating the local moonshiners he had personally known, often citing the locations of their operations and reminding Mama that certain of these practitioners were also our kin. It was difficult to refute him on such assertions, considering the extensive amount on-site research he had personally conducted.

It also upset Mama when Uncle John wrote about how Grandma would frequently take long arduous hikes from her home on Mayberry Road, all the way up through Kettle Hollow and on up to the highest point in Mayberry, the top of the hill called Hurricane Knob. According to my uncle, she would make that demanding trek at least once a week, sometimes more often, if the weather was nice. Grandma was a rather heavy woman who chronically limped because of painful bunions, so climbing to the top of that knob had to have been something of an ordeal for her. The trail up the knob was rough and steep and the knob is called "The Hurricane" for good reason. And it is true that, once she had made the climb, she would spend an inordinate amount of time up there, in spite of the wind and the rough terrain.

Mama always insisted that Grandma made those trips up Hurricane Knob to visit the grave of her own mother, Ruth Barnard Reynolds. Her mother's grave is located in the Barnard Cemetery near the crest of that hill, but Grandma's time up there was not all spent in mourning at the cemetery. Uncle John claimed there was another reason why she made those trips so often. He thought that Grandma was investigating rumors she may have heard about a brother or a nephew or someone else she knew, someone who was rumored to have been making moonshine somewhere around Mayberry. Grandma knew the precise location of every occupied dwelling within the grand view from Hurricane

Knob, and she knew who lived where. From the knob, she could accurately judge whether any wisp of smoke that she might see drifting up from the woodlands below was coming from someone cooking supper or from some other source such as a still.

If Grandma spotted smoke coming up from out of the woods over near where her brother Leon or her nephew Carver had a piece of land, she might well have assumed that the smoke she saw was coming from a still. But Grandma was smart; instead of calling the Sheriff's Office and reporting the location right away, she would first try an implied threat. She apparently thought that she could make whomever was cooking up moonshine nervous enough that they just might shut down or move their still.

Uncle John once told of how, when he was a child, he overheard one end of a telephone conversation between Grandma and someone. Back in pre-WWII Mayberry, the telephones were big wooden boxes that hung on the wall and there was no such thing as a private conversation between those who were using them. Anyone speaking into the phone had to shout out loud if they were to be heard on the other end. From two rooms away, Uncle John could hear Grandma yelling into the telephone and telling her brother, "Leon, I been hearing people say that maybe you and Carver are makin' moonshine in them woods down on the Acey Spangler Branch again. Now, I told em' that I knowed it wasn't so, 'cause that's such an obvious place. Didn't the deputies chop up a still down there just a few years back? I'd bet that if anybody put a still down there now, it'd get busted up in no time." If her psychology failed, I expect that Grandma really would have notified the authorities; she truly hated booze, and she was mighty strong on her principles.

The moonshining activity in remote mountain communities such as Mayberry in the early twentieth century was a result of economic conditions more than anything else. For the first century of Mayberry's existence, there were few ways, other than hardscrabble farming, that anyone could make a living there. The main crop grown in Mayberry was corn, of course, and it was a lot easier to make a one day ride to town on the back of a mule while carrying a few gallons of liquid corn than it was to spend one full day hauling a wagon load of whole ears of corn down from the mountain to Stuart or Mount Airy and then returning home the next day. Corn liquor provided an especially appealing trade option at a time when a few jugs of moonshine would bring in more money than a wagon load of corn.

During Mayberry's early years, the only businesses that existed there were a general store, a grist mill, and a sawmill or two. Around the turn of the century, a tannery and a cobbler's shop were added, but those businesses provided employment for only a few. By the time of the Great Depression, the economy was back to where the only functioning businesses were the store and some timbering and sawmilling. Most of the breadwinners in Mayberry were farmers, and it is understandable that some of them became involved in moonshining just so they could earn a little cash.

The state of Virginia beat the Federal government to the punch when it enacted a state-wide prohibition on alcoholic spirits in 1914, but that altered the alcohol commerce in Mayberry hardly at all. When nation-wide prohibition came to an end in 1933, that didn't change the amount of moonshining in Mayberry very much either. There has never been an establishment in Mayberry, either before, during, or after prohibition, that sold alcohol legally, but that is definitely not to say that there was no alcohol available. Most of the folks in Mayberry heard about it when the constitutional amendment was passed that prohibited the manufacture and sale of alcoholic beverages, and a few years later they learned that the amendment had been repealed for some reason. But so far as the availability of the kind of booze commonly found in Mayberry was concerned, there were few changes. The same folks were making and drinking the same stuff in the same amounts, before prohibition, during prohibition, and following the repeal of prohibition.

It is often assumed that the only manufacture of alcohol that ever took place in the Blue Ridge Mountains was *illegal* moonshining, but that is not quite the case. There were over 250 federally licensed distilleries operating in Virginia in the years just prior to prohibition, and many of those distilleries were located in the Blue Ridge Mountains. There were even a couple of perfectly legal distilling operations located within a mile or two of Mayberry. Other than a federal tax stamp glued over the stopper of each bottle of liquor sold by those legal distilleries, however, there was little else that distinguished the legally distilled alcoholic products from the illegal ones.

One of those government licensed distilleries was located beside the Danville/Wytheville Pike near the Floyd County line. That corner of Patrick County was a part of the Mayberry, Virginia, postal route, back in the days when Mayberry had a post office and the main road was the Danville-Wytheville Pike instead of Highway 58. That made *Mayberry Creek*, Virginia, (no zip code then) the official postal address of the government licensed distillery operated by Mr. Bill Williams. It just happened that Mr. Williams was my great-grandfather on my father's side, and Great Granddaddy Bill Williams ran his government licensed distillery from about 1890 until 1914, when the advent of prohibition in the State of Virginia caused it to be shut down.

For some of the distilleries that were begun as government licensed operations, the biggest change introduced by prohibition was the necessity for the owners to move the distilling equipment from a still house conveniently located near a public road to a remote patch of woods somewhere near a stream. For many of the ornery Scots-Irish who populated much of Virginia at the time, having the government declare that the production and distribution of alcohol was now illegal just made the drinking of it more fun, and of course, it also made the distilling of it much more profitable.

The distance from Maple Swamp, where my maternal great grandfather Elam Reynolds and his family lived, to Bill Williams' government licensed distillery near the Danville/Wytheville Pike was less than a mile in 1900. I find it ironic and somewhat sad that, while my grandmother on one side of the family was signing petitions and writing her congressmen urging them to support prohibition, my great grandfather on the other side was legally selling booze to my prohibitionist grandmother's daddy. As a youngster, when I would hear Grandma tell her woeful tales about her father "going off over the hill to buy likker," I always imagined him just walking over to an illegal moonshine still being operated by a nearby neighbor. That probably happened too, but often enough, whenever my great grandfather Elam managed to get his hands on a little money, he would soon be hiking over the hill to pay a visit to Bill Williams.

I was just a young kid when I first learned that my great grandfather Bill Williams had operated a distillery. At the time, that knowledge caused me to wonder if the verse from the song about *That Good Ole Mountain Dew* that says "My Uncle Bill runs a still on the hill, where he runs off a gallon or two…" was written about my great grandfather.

During the early 1900's, years before prohibition and during a time when there was plenty of legal liquor available, many people would choose to drink illegal moonshine simply because it was a lot cheaper than the commercially made whiskey. The main reason for the difference in price between the legal and the illegal booze was of course, state and federal taxes. The price difference was most significant around the turn of the twentieth century, when the Federal Tax on a gallon of 100 proof whiskey was $1.10. The addition of the state tax brought the price of even the cheapest legally made booze up to almost two dollars per gallon, and this was at a time when a gallon of illegal moonshine could be bought in Mayberry for as little as fifty cents.

You may remember from history class that the government licensing of whiskey distilleries in the United States goes all the way back to 1791. Of course, that licensing had little to do with a government attempt to influence the morality of its people or even having an interest in the safety of the liquor they were drinking. The only purpose in the government's licensing of distilleries was to insure that the whisky produced was being taxed to provide the Nation's Government with revenue. For the first hundred years of the existence of Our Republic, the tax on alcohol was the Federal Government's major source of income. Needless to say, there were many Americans who were unhappy with the new tax on spirits, so the business known as moonshining had its beginnings in the newly formed United States with the introduction of the whisky tax. Some of the citizens of the New Republic were obviously violently opposed to this tax. Do you also remember being told about the Whiskey Rebellion, the insurrection in which the corn farmers of Pennsylvania took up arms against the Federal Government in opposition to the tax on whiskey? The farmers were afraid that the tax would shut down the liquor industry at a time when the liquor industry consumed most of the corn they produced. We have learned by now, however, that taxing a commodity has little effect on the amount of it that is sold.

As soon as the law creating the whisky tax was passed, the Federal Government found it necessary to impose penalties for engaging in the manufacture and sale of untaxed whisky. This, in turn, created the need to employ individuals called "revenuers" to go around searching for persons engaging in the now illegal unlicensed whisky related activities. So, just in case the meaning of terms such as *moonshining* and *moonshiner* are not self-evident to everyone, the names began to be applied to illegally made spirits and its makers on the assumption that, since the activity was now illegal, much of the unlicensed distilling of spirits was now taking place at night and with assistance from the light of the moon.

With the beginning of prohibition, all of the revenue generated by the whiskey excise tax immediately went away, but the money required to run the government, build roads and bridges, fight wars, etc. had to come from somewhere. That was when the modern version of our Federal Income Tax was created. You are probably aware that the Federal Income Tax did not go away following the repeal of prohibition, however.

Here in the South, it is often assumed that the term *moonshine* primarily applies to illegally manufactured ***corn liquor***. In reality though, there are many different forms of moonshine, although the "illegal" part is generally correct. In states where a lot of fruit, especially apples and peaches, was grown, the amount of brandy produced often exceeded the amount of corn liquor. Prior to prohibition, the small legal distilleries would often produce both corn liquor (the quintessential "moonshine" whiskey), and also brandy made from whatever fruit happened to be in season. Some of the distillery licenses issued in pre-prohibition Virginia were valid for only three months each fall, the months coinciding with the apple harvest.

For years now, much of the moonshine folks have bought under the assumption that it was illegal *corn* liquor has been made from any of a host of other ingredients. While it is true that today there is a lot of unaged corn liquor being legally made and sold under the label of "moonshine," much of the illegal moonshine in the years not so far past was made with only some corn (or possibly no corn) used as an ingredient. When corn is in short supply, there are always plenty of substitutes, including several kinds of commercially available animal feed.

For the moonshiner in a big hurry to get some liquor to market, the simplest form of moonshine can be made from fermenting and distilling a mash consisting of plain old table sugar and bakers' yeast mixed with water and whatever. The "whatever" can be sprouted corn (good), barley malt (also good), wheat middlings (awful), and any of a host of other potential ingredients. After the mash has been distilled, more sugar and water can be added to the whatever, and the mash fermented and distilled again. The process can be repeated a number of times, with each successive batch being worse than the one before. This form of moonshine is generally recognized as the lowest grade produced, other than some really, really bad and toxic varieties made that include embalming fluid, denatured alcohol, etc.

I once stood by and watched as a fellow from Mayberry turned up a fruit jar and took a big swallow of the moonshine that he himself had just recently made. He gargled and sputtered a bit, and it took him an alarming amount of time for him to regain his breath. "Whew," he wheezed, when he could finally speak. "Awful, just awful. They oughta' be a law agin' makin' ol' sugar likker."

I had long assumed that my great grandfather's legal distillery mostly made white corn liquor – the unaged corn liquor that most people associate with the term "mountain dew" – but I later learned that Bill Williams also made apple brandy and that he even aged some of the fruit liquor for a few years. Although Mr. Williams owned a substantial apple orchard of his own, his brandy was in such demand that he sometimes imported wagon loads of apples bought from orchards over near Wytheville. He also had a storage shed with two sturdy locks on the door. He kept the key for one of the locks, but the other lock had to be opened by a government official. At that time, the shed with two locks met the minimum legal requirement for it to function as a bonded whiskey warehouse.

Federal tax agents would periodically come by to check on the Williams Distillery's production of liquor and insure that the proper amount of federal tax was being paid. There is a family story about how Mr. Williams, having previously hidden a personal stash of brandy under the hay in his barn loft, became concerned that the authorities inspecting the premises might detect his personal stash from the smell. He brought two bottles of his brandy with him, presumably for the agents' to examine, as he accompanied them on their inspection tour. As the group approached the barn where his stash was hidden, Great Grandpa feigned a stumble and dropped one of the bottles he was carrying onto a rock. That happened to be the only rock of any significance anywhere near his barn, but the bottle was shattered and its contents dispersed. Any whiff of brandy that the inspectors might have detected near that barn could then have been attributed to the brandy from the bottle that had just been broken.

Like all other legal distilleries in Virginia, Bill Williams' legal distilling operation came to an end in 1914, when the state of Virginia enacted its own prohibition law, six years before the Volstead Act instituted prohibition nationwide. Mr. Williams, however, seemed to have stashed enough of his product away to satisfy his own personal needs for a very long time. My dad liked to talk about how, back in the nineteen thirties, his Granddad Williams would keep a bottle of brandy hidden in the boxwood beside the front door of his home. Dad said that he never saw his grandpa give the slightest indication that he had imbibed any alcohol, but that his grandpa did consider an occasional snort of brandy to be an effective dose of preventive medicine.

Even though Great Grandmother never expressed any objection to Great Grandad making and selling the stuff – perhaps because she appreciated the income it provided – she was so strongly opposed to Great Grandpa ever drinking any of what he had made, that he had to take his libations on the sly. Dad described how his grandpa, upon leaving his house, would walk out onto the front porch and down the steps. But while going down the steps, he could reach down into the boxwood and retrieve a hidden bottle. He could pull the stopper out of the bottle, take a swallow, then close the bottle up and replace it in the boxwood while never slowing his pace or missing a step.

Moonshining in Mayberry was probably at its peak in the mid-nineteen thirties, before experiencing a declining in the years following the Second World War. Even as late as the fifties, however, an older cousin told me that he knew of four operating stills that were accessible along a two-mile length of road between the Parkway near Mayberry and Highway 58. This cousin was someone who would have known what he was talking about when it came to moonshine in Mayberry. By the nineteen sixties, I knew of just two moonshiners who were operating near Mayberry, and they were both getting on in years at the time. So far as I can tell, there has been little moonshine made in and around Mayberry for the last couple of decades. I think that has to do with both changes in taste and in economics.

When you get right down to basics, real moonshine is simply not very good to many peoples' taste. The quality tends to be pretty unreliable, and most of us are aware that imbibing a significant amount over any extended period of time can be really rough on one's constitution. As the economy improved and the folks who drank could afford something better, they started drinking "red" liquor or maybe even wine, and they pretty much abandoned corn liquor. It has been several years since anyone offered to sell me any "real" moonshine, and he wanted ten dollars for a pint back then. I think that price was comparable to the price of the lower grades of the legal and less hazardous stuff available from the government regulated ABC stores.

One of the things that discourages anyone from going into the business of moonshining today is the fact that making liquor requires a lot of hard work. When factory jobs started coming to the area in the forties and the fifties, those wages were about as much as someone could make from moonshining, the factory work was not as demanding, and a factory worker did not have to worry about getting arrested.

Now that so many of the factory jobs have gone away, will moonshining be coming back? It already has in a way, given the increasing number of entrepreneurs who are now opening legal "moonshine" distilleries in The Carolinas and Virginia. But that is not really the same thing, is it? Anyway, even for someone who is underemployed, drinking cheap beer is a lot easier and safer than building and cranking up a still to make your own version of moonshine liquor.

One reason I wanted to write about the moonshining around Mayberry, Virginia, is that I think that Mayberry, as a somewhat remote mountain community, is just the kind of place where a visitor might expect to find a little moonshining going on. It is definitely true that just a couple of generations ago, there was "quite a bit" of moonshine being made in the area. That "quite a bit" of moonshine, however, is relative. For as far back as anyone can remember, there were folks in Mayberry who were making a little illegal liquor now and then, but there were never any large commercial quantities being produced there. The amount of illegal booze made in Mayberry has always been pretty insignificant when compared to the amount produced in locations better known for their moonshining, places such as Wilkes County, North Carolina, or Franklin County, Virginia.

After all, Wilkes County is just a few miles from some good-sized towns such as Winston Salem and Raleigh, and Franklin County has customer bases conveniently located in nearby towns such as Roanoke and Lynchburg. Mayberry is not very close to any large town, so most of the moonshine distilled here in Mayberry has always been primarily for local consumption. I guess you could say that "whatever was made in Mayberry, stayed in Mayberry."

Ol' Arm Stretcher

Great Uncle Leon could be described as a man who possessed most of the vices and the virtues often attributed to the stereotypical mountain man of his day. He made, drank, and sold moonshine liquor, and while he was not keen on working too hard himself, he demanded that his wife and children always "keep their noses to the grindstone." Even as his family was struggling to keep body and soul together, Uncle Leon's passions in life continued to be hunting and fishing, playing the fiddle, and spending a lot of time drinking and swapping tall tales with his cronies. Sometimes, without actually calling him out by name, Grandma would use her brother as an example of what a man should never aspire to be, as she would moralize to her grandchildren about how being well respected is so much more important than being well liked. Her favorite case in point was to tell us that, while a moonshiner might be well liked by his customers, he was really just a scoff-law who was not well respected by solid, law-abiding folks such as herself. I must have been about ten or eleven when it became clear to me that the individual she was using as an example was actually a member of the family.

Uncle Leon was a large, portly man with a bountiful shock of white hair and a booming bass voice that made him a looming presence anywhere he might be. He could claim a respectable level of proficiency in several occupations, including veterinarian, land surveyor, and horse-trader. The pursuits that appeared to have served him best, however, were two part-time endeavors that complemented each other. He would often serve the county as a part-time game warden, and he would also conduct auctions in which he presided as the auctioneer. This combination enabled him to work the system in some creative ways.

Uncle Leon was known to have dabbled in the manufacturing end of the moonshine industry for a few years when he was still youthful and energetic, but as he became older and much heavier, he decided that making it was such hard work that he would just concentrate on the retail end of the business. Even at that, he preferred to not be involved in anything so crude as simply maintaining a supply of booze and selling it to anyone who might walk up and want to buy. Uncle Leon found it more profitable and less risky to use moonshine as a premium to assist in the promotion of his other endeavors.

My great uncle was a connoisseur of illegal hooch, if there is such a thing, and his early association with the manufacturing end of the business probably did give him some insight into the methods and materials that produced spirits of superior quality. He made a serious effort to cultivate amiable relations with the moonshiners he knew, especially those whom he judged to produce a finer grade of spirits.

One of Uncle Leon's many endeavors was the provision of guide services for weekend outdoorsmen who would come up to the mountains to hunt and fish. His good relations with local moonshiners helped to insure that he would always have plenty of superior grade illegal liquor available to share with his clients.

The time Uncle Leon spent patrolling the local woodlands and streams in his job as a game warden also meant that he developed excellent insight into the best places to take his clients on hunting and fishing expeditions. It was alleged that he was not above using his authority as a game warden to pressure competitors to seek fishing streams and hunting grounds in areas that were less bountiful than those to which he intended to guide his own clients.

During the time of prohibition, game wardens such as Uncle Leon were often recruited by government agencies to assist Federal and State Law Enforcement Officers in their less-than-enthusiastic campaign against the manufacture of illegal liquor. The assumption was that their work as game wardens should allow them to become especially familiar with locations where stills were likely to be concealed. Some folks thought that Leon was likely to have led the Agents to distilleries whose operators provided the moonshine for his competitors and diverted law enforcement away from his own suppliers, but these were only speculations.

Whenever it became necessary for a Mayberry family to dispose of their estate, the home, farm, and other worldly possessions, Leon Reynolds was usually the person called upon to perform the delicate and sometimes depressing business. Often, when Leon was conducting an estate auction, he would employ the time-honored strategy of maintaining a supply of free alcohol for the benefit of potential bidders. The obvious theory behind such a practice was that the resulting impairment of the bidders' judgments could mean that he would obtain premium prices for the items being auctioned. The reliable results obtained for the sellers at the auctions he conducted doubtlessly enhanced his reputation as an auctioneer and stimulated a demand for his services. Even folks who knew perfectly well what Leon was up to could not resist the enticement of good free hooch. Often, they would decide to attend an auction in which they would otherwise have had little interest. I have heard many stories about how folks who were attending an auction conducted by Leon Reynolds somehow found themselves to be the proud owners of items for which they had paid a fine price and for which they had little use.

There is even a family story about how Uncle Leon took advantage of the husband of his own recently married niece at one of his estate auctions. Uncle Dub and Aunt Alice had been married for only about a year when the estate of a once well-to-do Mayberry family was put up for sale. The widow who had owned the home and farm had recently passed away, and she and her husband had owned a lot of stuff. There was the house, the land and farm buildings, plus the furniture, the farm machinery, and all the many things the family had accumulated through the many years of their marriage, but like most mountain folk, they never accumulated a lot of money. Their children had no desire to try earning their livings on that mountain farm, and they had all moved away years before. Now, the surviving children just wanted to sell every last thing their parents had owned for as much money as they could get. The country was still trying to recover from the depression, and even in the best of times, there was no way all of the heirs in a farm family could earn their livings on a mountain farm that had to be split five ways. As so often happened, the land, the house, and everything the deceased had owned was put up for auction, with Uncle Leon as the auctioneer.

In preparation for the auction, Leon had obtained a couple of gallons of what was described by those in attendance as some excellent locally-made apple brandy. He had stashed it in the barn ahead of time and had hired a couple of "assistants" to mingle with the crowd before the auction started, offering samples to potential bidders. The assistants were also instructed to pay attention to how the auction was going, and the more an individual might bid, the more often he should be offered additional samples in appreciation. Uncle Dub was targeted early in the auction, and he readily succumbed to the temptation. Being someone who rarely drank alcohol, my uncle soon found himself in pretty wobbly condition.

I think it is a fair assumption that the auctioneer directed his helpers to target Dub Hoskins. Uncle Leon was likely to have known that one of the items to be auctioned was a cherry wood corner cupboard that had once belonged to Aunt Alice's grandmother, and he could well have assumed that Aunt Alice had her mind set on getting that piece of fine antique furniture back into the family. Uncle Leon also knew that Uncle Dub's business in Stuart was doing quite well, at least by depression standards, and he could also have guessed that Dub and his new wife were still in the process of setting up housekeeping and would be looking for items with which to furnish their home. Leon Reynolds often asked around and sought out advance information about folks he thought might be bidding in an upcoming auction, and he was especially interested in family connections. This was just good business, and learning about such useful connections was not difficult in a small gossipy community like Mayberry, where almost everyone was related to almost everyone else.

The auctioneer was spot on for that day. Aunt Alice had indeed sent her husband to the auction with specific instructions to try to buy the cherry wood corner cupboard and also to buy a walnut bedroom suite that she thought was likely to be up for auction. That was all she expected her husband to buy, however.

Almost as soon as the auction started, Uncle Dub jumped right in and started bidding on stuff. He bought cupboards and tables and chairs and a couple of bedroom suits, and while he did buy the particular items that Aunt Alice had wanted, he also bought a whole lot more. Although he and his wife could have used most of the furniture he bought, he also ended up with a couple of old muzzle loading rifles, a corn sheller, an egg incubator, a corn planter, a plowing harness, a hand powered water pump, and a whole bunch of other farm tools and equipment. Uncle Dub didn't even have a farm.

My dad, who was also at the auction, said even after

most of the large items had been sold and the bidders had begun to drift away, Uncle Dub continued to stand right in front of the auctioneer's podium, so wobbly that he was supporting himself by leaning on the two antique rifles he had bought. He had a horse collar hanging around his neck, a World War I vintage Army helmet cocked up on his head, and he was bidding on just about everything that came up, right until the very end.

Dub had driven a truck to the auction, an indication that he might buy a lot of stuff, but by the end of the auction, he was in no condition to drive anything. That was when Dub's brother-in-law, Hassell Yeatts, and my dad got together to figure out how they could get a besotted Uncle Dub and his many purchases safely back to Stuart. Even the truck that Dub had driven to the auction could not carry everything he had bought, so my dad borrowed a second truck. While Dad and Uncle Hassell were loading up the two trucks, Uncle Dub climbed into the cab of his truck and went sound asleep.

It took quite a while to get everything loaded and secured, so it was almost dark by the time they were headed down the mountain to Stuart. Just before they got to Stuart, Uncle Dub woke up and looked around in a daze. When he asked Hassell why he was driving his truck, Hassell explained about the brandy and how Dub was judged to be in no shape to drive anything, especially a truck that was loaded down with all of the stuff that he had bought.

"All what stuff? Did I buy a lot of stuff?" Uncle Dub was completely befuddled.

"You bought everything that's in the back of this truck," Hassell told him.

Dub leaned out of the window, turning his head and looking back, trying to see into the bed of his truck. That was when Hassell told him, "You bought all the stuff that's on that truck following us too."

"Oh my God," Dub moaned as he turned back inside in the truck and slid down in the seat. "I can't take all this stuff home. Alice will kill me. Pull over when you get a chance."

Hassell pulled the truck off to the side of the road on the outskirts of Stuart and Dad pulled in behind him. At Uncle Dub's direction, instead of hauling all the things he had bought to his house, they stashed most of it in a downtown storage building that Dub used for his business. In fact, the only item that was delivered to Dub and Alice's home that night was the cherry corner cupboard he was instructed to buy in the first place.

The story does have a happy ending. Uncle Dub wisely kept all of the rest of his auction loot stashed away in his storage building, slyly bringing an item home when there was a special occasion such as Aunt Alice's birthday or their anniversary. Usually, Alice was pleased. As for the farm equipment, Dub would sell a piece every now and then to someone who had a use for it, and he may have nearly broken even on all that. The muzzle loading rifles that he bought for ten dollars apiece were a different matter. His sons still have them, and by now they must have a value of several hundred dollars each. Uncle Leon may have done his nephew-in-law a big favor in the long term.

Great Uncle Leon would sometimes laugh and freely admit that he was guilty of providing free booze at the auctions he conducted, even acknowledging that it was provided for the express purpose of impairing the judgment of potential bidders and loosening their purse strings. He liked to refer to the free hooch he would provide as “Old Arm Stretcher.”

“There are always folks at auctions who have deep pockets,” he would say, “but some of ‘em have awfully short arms. All I do is give them a dose of that ‘old arm stretcher,’ so they can reach way down deep into those pockets. It’s not like I’m twistin’ their arms, I’m just stretching ‘em a little, so they can reach a little bit deeper.”

A month or two after the auction, Uncle Dub confided to my dad that he had made a pledge to never ever attend another auction run by Leon Reynolds, and that he had also pledged to never ever take another drink of moonshine. I’m pretty sure that both of those were pledges that he kept.

I see that the cost of living has gone up another dollar a quart. W.C. Fields

Cozy Corner

Not long after Franklin D. Roosevelt was inaugurated as the Nation's President in 1933, folks in Mayberry began hearing rumors that the Government was going to be funding two big public works projects that were likely to have a major impact on their community. Dump Yeatts and his son Coy took those rumors seriously enough that in 1934, they bought the old Mayberry Store, a small general store that had been closed down for almost six years by then. They reopened it in 1935, and their purchase soon proved to have been a shrewd decision.

In that same year, the two biggest construction projects in the history of the area got underway. First there was the City of Danville Hydroelectric Project, a government financed public works project in which two dams and an electric power generation plant were to be built in the Dan River George near Mayberry. Then, before the Dan River Hydroelectric Project had been completed, the construction of the Blue Ridge Parkway was begun. That scenic highway runs through the Blue Ridge Mountains from the Shenandoah National Park in northern Virginia to the Smoky Mountain National Park in southwestern North Carolina, and the route of that new four-hundred mile long Parkway passed right through Mayberry. For the second half of the 1930's, the community of Mayberry enjoyed a level of economic prosperity that it has never experienced, before or since, even as most of the country continued to struggle through the Great Depression.

When those projects got under way in Mayberry, jobs suddenly became available for any able-bodied men who wanted to work, with pay that was several times the prevailing local wages.

In addition, anyone in Mayberry who had a room (or even a barn loft or a shed) that they were willing to rent out as housing for project workers could also have had some additional of income. During 1937 and 1938, for example, my grandmother was renting out rooms to four Danville Project workers at the same time. She charged each of the workers five dollars a week for room and board which included a bed shared by two plus breakfast and dinner. For another dollar a week, she would provide a worker with packed lunches for six days.

With the influx of all those workers who had good jobs and cash to spend, every store in the area experienced a dramatic increase in business. The projects were especially beneficial to the Mayberry Store, which was located near the center of Mayberry and right beside one of the main roads connecting Highway 58 to the project construction sites. The Mayberry Store was also located just a hundred yards from the proposed route of the new Blue Ridge Parkway through Mayberry. But of course. the Mayberry store would not remain the only general store in the community for very long.

About a mile south of Mayberry proper and less than a mile north of site where one of the dams across the Dan River was being constructed, the Hydroelectric Works Project contractor, Chas T. Main, built a long, narrow, tarpaper covered building to serve as barracks for some of the hydroelectric project workers who had temporarily relocated to Mayberry. Many of the workers found the comfort of the beds and the quality of the food they experienced when boarding in private homes in the community to be outstanding, but there were simply not enough spare rooms and probably not enough good cooks for all of the workers to enjoy such facilities.

A local businessman named Ed Hylton just happened to own a couple of acres of land right next to where the Mayberry Road connected with the new road leading down to the site of the lower dam. That plot of land was within easy walking distance of the Project Workers' Barracks, and Ed knew an opportunity when he saw one. Reasoning that all of these new temporary residents would be in need of a lot of basic items such as soft drinks, chewing tobacco, and razor blades, he opened another little general store right beside that intersection.

The location of the new store was a mile closer to the Dam Project than the Mayberry Store, and Mr. Hylton could see no reason why the Mayberry Store should be the only business benefiting from the Government Projects. He also reasoned that most of the clientele for his store were going to be there for only a few years, so there was no need to build any elaborate kind of structure. His new store was housed in a squat, hastily constructed wooden shed covered with tar paper. Modest signs were nailed onto either side of the front of the store, with one to the left of the door that simply announced "STORE" in white hand-painted letters. To the right of the door, there was a red metal sign that held a thermometer and was emblazoned with a script version of the words “Coca Cola.” The little store was located right beside one of the main roads leading to the project site, and it was overwhelmed with customers from the day it first opened.

There was no electric power available in Mayberry in those days, but the new store was doing such a great business that the owner soon invested in a Homelite gasoline powered generator to provide electricity for his new business. It was kind of expensive to run a gasoline powered generator a whole lot, so Ed would usually run it for just a few hours each day. At first, the owner did not even keep the place open after dark, so the original function of the generator was not to light up the store at night. The generator was mostly run in the afternoons, charging the batteries that were used to power the single bulb suspended from the ceiling near the middle of the store and the drink cooler that sat behind the counter. In the summers especially, there was a definite need to have plenty of cold soda pop for the workers coming up from their long, hot day of working on the dam down in the Dan River Gorge.

Almost as soon as the store was opened, a few of the workers who were from places other than Mayberry began sidling up to the proprietor and confidentially asking, “Do you know where can I get something to drink?” At first, Ed’s standard reply was, “Well, I got a great big cooler back here, and its plumb full of Co-Cola, Orange Crush, and Seven-up.”

“Nah, I’m looking for something besides pop,” was a typical response to Mr. Ed’s offerings. “Can’t a feller even get a beer around here someplace?”

Mr. Ed reluctantly gave out the names of a couple of local bootleggers, but he had no interest in getting involved with any illegal booze business himself. While he was still in the process of building the place, he had been approached by the project superintendent. The Super had let him know that it would be best if the men working on the dam didn't have access to spirits, and he had said outright that if he found that an establishment was selling any bootlegged liquor to his men, he would get it shut down in a hurry. But then the superintendent had added that he knew that many of the workers would like to have a cold beer after work sometimes, and he understood that. That should create no problem with worker reliability, Ed and he agreed, since any beer sold legally in the State of Virginia at that time could contain no more than 3.2 percent alcohol.

National Prohibition had been repealed just two years before, but that did not mean that the sale of beer in Mayberry or anywhere else in Patrick County had yet become legal. The sale of beer anywhere in Virginia required a license from both the county and the state, and in many localities, the licensing of establishments to sell any kind of alcoholic beverage was prevented by the combined influence of local religious leaders and some of the bootleggers who were continuing to profit from local prohibition laws. That was true for all of Patrick and other nearby Counties, and it was especially true of small communities such as Mayberry and Meadows of Dan.

Ed knew that Mr. Yeatts at the Mayberry Store was unlikely to even try to get a license to sell beer, so he figured that if he could somehow manage to sell a little beer at his own place, it would really give him a leg up on the competition. He also knew that if he applied for a license, it would probably be a year or two before he could get one. He would have to go through the county and the state governments, and that would be sure to generate a lot of opposition. He thought it likely that the license would be denied anyway, so he might just as well take a short cut. He made an arrangement for someone who went to Wytheville every week to pick up a few cases of beer for him while he was there and deliver them to his store.

Ed put the beer in a second cooler hidden in the stock room, assuming that if he kept everything low key, he wouldn't have to worry about local law enforcement coming in and shutting him down. He told his customers to please drink their beer indoors or at least keep it out of sight of folks passing by on the road. Even though his customers did not always honor that request, there must not have been many complaints, because he never did have any problems with the local law enforcement.

The little store was doing so well that the owner began to think about expanding right away. He thought about all of those men working in Mayberry, having to stay away from their homes and families all week with no entertainment available in the evenings. Some on the men even stayed on in Mayberry over the weekends, and surely they needed a place where they could have a little fun. He had set up some horseshoe stakes out behind the store, and on warm evenings and weekends, there were men waiting in line for their turn at throwing horseshoes. Sometimes, they were still trying to throw those horseshoes after it was too dark to see from one stake to the other!

Ed thought that maybe he should provide some more recreation for those men, recreation for which he could charge a small fee of course. Maybe he should add a building that was large enough to hold a couple of pool tables. Then he could get an electric power generator large enough to light up both buildings and provide power for the really big beer cooler that he would put inside the pool building. The first thing folks in Mayberry knew, Ed had thrown up a second building right beside the first one, similar in its tarpaper covered construction but almost twice as long. The new building was long enough to hold three pool tables, another beer cooler, and a juke box. It became a really busy place in the evenings up until nine o'clock. The project superintendent had already told Mr. Ed that he thought nine would be a reasonable closing time.

Not everyone was happy with all the new commercial development in Mayberry. A lot of Mayberry folks had no use for either pool or beer, and some thought that respectable citizens of Mayberry should not be seen anywhere near Ed's business establishments.

Although the signs on the first building that said "STORE" and "Coca-Cola, were still in place, a sign on the newer building displayed the word "BILLARDS" in foot-high letters. There were also a lot of new signs that suddenly appeared all over both buildings. They advertised merchandise such as Camel Cigarettes, Bull Durham Chewing Tobacco, and Baby Ruth Candy Bars, but Mayberry folks hadn't seen anything yet!

No one can remember for sure if the name Cozy Corner was given to the little retail development before or after the construction of the mysterious third building. The third building was thrown up almost overnight, and it was located on the other side of the road from the pool hall. Although it was of similar construction to the other two, building number three was different from the others in that it had a couple of small windows on the front side and two more windows on the back. The windows were all placed high up on the walls for some reason, and they had curtains and shades that were always closed.

The main door of the third building had a small sign stating "PRIVATE CLUB" tacked onto it, whatever that was supposed to mean. After that, everyone began referring to Ed's third economic enterprise as "Cozy Corner," and it didn't take long for observant folks to become suspicious about some of its functions. Mr. Ed called it a recreation hall (for members only) and claimed that it wasn't even his building. It was true that Building Number Three had been built on property owned by somebody else, but Mr. Ed sure appeared to be the manager.

There didn't seem to be much going on at that building during the week, and the shades on the inside of the little windows were kept pulled down. The real oddity, however, was the large number of persons of the female persuasion that began to be seen hanging around at Cozy Corner on the weekends. This was especially strange because most of the Women of Mayberry were reluctant to be seen anywhere near Ed's store or pool room, seeing as how he sold beer and had pool tables and everything like that. And there were no women at all employed at the Danville Project Construction Site in Mayberry, so who were these ladies?

The women who were seen slinking around Cozy Corner Building #3 did not look like they were from anywhere near Mayberry. Most of the women of Mayberry were hard-working farm women who wore plain print dresses that reached down to the tops of their shoes and they usually had kerchiefs or sun bonnets on their heads. The women seen around Cozy Corner wore fancy clothes with skirts that barely came down to their knees; they had bobbed hair and wore lip rouge, and their faces and hands showed no indication that they ever worked outside in the sun. Most of the women appeared to be rather pale, as far as one could tell through all that makeup. Was it possible that Mayberry had its first-time-ever, sure-enough, professionally-staffed house of ill repute?

Although most of the folks in Mayberry were thankful that the times were finally getting better, there were some things about these new developments that were causing a lot of concern for some Mayberry residents. One person with a special concern was Zuby Bowden, a Mayberry woman with a worried mind. She had not been any too pleased when her husband Doster began coming home after work on Saturdays smelling like he'd been drinking beer. This was the first job Doster ever had that paid good wages, and everyone knew that the Danville Project was only going to last for three or four years. Most of the country was still in a depression, and practical-minded women like Zuby thought that they should be squirreling away every penny of those good project wages that they could. Folks around Mayberry were always saying things like "hard times will be back soon enough."

The Danville Project workers put in half of a workday on most Saturdays, and then they would get their weekly pay that afternoon. Not all of the workers were dismissed at the same time on Saturday, however. Otherwise, they would all have been lined up at the paymasters shack for hours. A group of workers would be dismissed every half-hour throughout the afternoon. The hourly workers got paid in cash, but the salaried workers got a check every week, and those checks had to be cashed somewhere. That payroll system worked well for both Cozy Corner and the Mayberry Store. A project truck would shuttle a group of workers up out of the gorge about every half hour on Saturday afternoons, so the workers who needed to cash checks were not all coming in at the same time.

Then, for a second or maybe a third time, after Doster had come home for lunch on a Saturday afternoon, he had cleaned himself up and then announced that he had to go back to Cozy Corner to get his check cashed.

"How come you didn't get that check cashed on the way home?" Zuby wanted to know.

"Well, there were so many of the men waiting in line at Cozy Corner, I bet I would have had to wait an hour or maybe two. I was getting really hungry." Zuby just didn't buy what Doster claimed.

Zuby wasn't stupid. She thought it strange that Doster would shave and wash up real good before he went back to Cozy Corner just to cash his check. Once she even caught him splashing on some of that smell-good shaving lotion before he left. Doster would tell Zuby that he might shoot a couple games of pool while he was at Cozy Corner and that he might even have a beer or two. Zuby felt that she shouldn't complain too much about that. She admitted that Doster deserved to have a little fun on a Saturday, considering how hard he worked all week. But it seemed to Zuby that it took Doster an awful long time to get his check cashed, even allowing time for a couple games of pool. It also looked to her like he might even be bringing home a little less pay than he had when he first started working at the Project for a salary.

Then came the Saturday evening when Doster came home late from Cozy Corner and Zuby caught a little whiff of some strange smelling perfume over the smell of Doster's beer and shaving lotion. Then she heard some of the neighbors gossiping about those "Danville Women" the girls hanging around Cozy Corner. When she was told about these strange, brazen, painted women that were sometimes seen lingering around the store and the pool room on weekends, that was when Zuby got real suspicious. A neighbor shared with Zuby that she had heard about how some of those strange women had been seen going into building number three accompanied by workmen from the project, and that could mean only one thing.

Although the rumors about Cozy Corner were flying all around Mayberry, most folks thought they couldn't all be true, and everybody was sure that Mr. Hylton was a fine upstanding citizen. On the other hand, Mayberry had been through some really tough times these past few years, and you couldn't blame a feller for wanting to get as much out of the recent surge of prosperity as he possibly could.

Zuby decided that some further investigation into this Cozy Corner business was definitely needed. She thought that maybe she had better go and see if pool was all that Doster was playing at this Cozy Corner place, even though she reckoned that her Doster would never succumb to the temptation of any of those Danville women. She was almost sure he wouldn't, but the very next Saturday, when Doster left the house to go back to the store and get his check cashed, Zuby was not that far behind.

It was just a little over a mile from Zuby and Doster's

little farm to Cozy Corner, and since Zuby did not want anyone see her going to that place anyway, she cut off some of the distance by walking across fields and through the woods. By cutting across Lincoln Light's hay field, she figured she could sneak up to the woods across the road from the Cozy Corner Store without being seen. And just as she had figured, after Zuby had crossed that field and walked through a little patch of woods, she came out right behind building number three. By then it was about three thirty on that Saturday afternoon, and just a trickle of workers was coming up the road from the dam site, some of them walking and some riding in a company truck. Several of them went inside to get their paychecks cashed, and with so many of the workers queued up at the counter inside, Zuby had no idea how long she might have to wait.

A lot of the workers soon climbed back onto the truck and were shuttled away from Cozy Corner. They were probably anxious to get home and maybe even get in a little work on their own farms before dark. But there was another group, mostly younger men who appeared to be from some place besides Mayberry, who didn't appear to be in any hurry to leave. Zuby thought those might be the guys she had heard about who were staying in the barracks. Most of them drifted in and out of the building that had the "BILLARDS" sign, and Zuby noticed that many of them were holding bottles of beer. When a couple of the men left the group and disappeared into building number three, there was a lot of joking and laughing exchanged among the others. Zuby moved down the road from building number three and sat down on a stump. From there she could also watch all of the goings on across the road at the store and the pool room. She sat on that stump for a long time, feeling more uneasy all the time, and she still had not seen any sign of Doster.

Finally, after about an hour, Doster came out of the pool room, but he didn't do much mingling with the other workmen. Just as soon as he started standing outside the poolroom drinking his beer, this strange woman walked up to him and they began talking. She stood up close to Doster, up real close, like she might be a real good friend of his. Then that brazen woman kind of nuzzled up to Doster, right out there in front of everybody, and it wasn't long before Doster was walking across the road with his right hand wrapped around a bottle of beer and his left arm wrapped around the waist of some woman who surely must have been one of those Danville hussies. It looked to Zuby like the two of them went into building number three.

Zuby's worst suspicions were now confirmed. Her first impulse was to rush screaming and cussin' over to the building where her Doster and the hussy had disappeared, kick down the door, and whip both of their sorry asses. But as she got up from her seat on the stump, a more devious plan began to form in her head. She walked back through the woods to a shock of hay she had passed as she crossed the field to get there. She gathered up an armload of hay and carried it through the woods to the back of building number three, and pushed it up against the wall. No one could see her from the store or pool hall, as she made that trip four or five times, transporting hay from the field and piling it against the back of the building. Finally, she brushed the hay from off her dress, straightened up tall, and walked around building number three and across the road to the front of the Cozy Corner store. She casually strolled through the door and up to the owner, who was standing behind the counter.

"Howdy Mr. Ed, have you seen my Doster today?" she asked him.

"Why no, Zuby," he lied. "Do you reckon he might be working overtime?"

"Well, if you see him, tell him I was here, but now I've gone home to fix supper," Zuby responded, calm as she could manage. Then she added, "Uh, Mr. Ed, would you gimme a pack of them Lucky Strike cigarettes?"

"And I do need a book of matches," she added.

It never occurred to Ed that he had never seen Zuby smoke, as Zuby plunked her dime down on the counter and he tossed out the pack of Lucky Strikes along with a paper book of matches. "Thank you kindly, Mr. Ed," said Zuby, as she picked up the cigarettes and matches and strolled out the door. But as soon as she was outside, Zuby made a quick turn and slipped down along the side of the pool hall. Then she scurried across the road to the far end of building number three and sneaked around to the back.

Zuby squatted down next to the mound of hay she had piled against the back of the number three, struck a match and held it under the bottom edge of the hay pile. As some of the hay caught fire, Zuby piled more handfuls of hay onto the blaze and then fanned it with her skirt. The whole pile of hay flared up to a healthy blaze in a few seconds. In about another minute, the tar paper covering on the back side of the building had caught fire, and soon the whole back of the building was burning vigorously.

Zuby stepped back from the fire and admired her handiwork for a moment, but then she felt a wave of panic when she realized how fast the fire was spreading. That's when she ran around the building and back across the road to the store. She stuck her head in through the door and hollered, "Mr. Ed, I think they's a fire goin' on out here somewheres. I can smell smoke real strong."

Zuby left the store and crossed back over the road, running past the burning building and into the woods to begin her walk back home. But then she could not resist stopping in the edge of the woods and turning back around to watch.

Ed had not been too alarmed by Zuby's announcement about the smell of smoke at first, so he didn't go out of the store to investigate until he heard someone hollering that building number three was on fire. By the time Ed got outside, one worker was beating on the front door of the burning building shouting for everyone to get out quick while some other men were trying to put out the fire.

Zuby was watching from the woods when the back door of building number three flew open and several courtesans and their customers, Doster and his friend among them, all in various stages of dress, came running out of the building. In spite of the obvious situations of the people leaving the building, she felt great relief when it appeared to her that everyone had gotten out.

Alas, there was not much water available at Cozy Corner, certainly not enough to deal with a fire that was burning the way that tarpaper covered building was. It was a long way down the hill to the spring, so the only water available was the water from the rain barrel, the bucket of drinking water from the store, and the water in the drink coolers. There were a few half-filled wash basins inside building number three, but nobody bothered with those.

The water, all combined, was woefully insufficient to put out the fire, and it wasn't more than five minutes until building number three was given up for lost. Then everybody began concentrating on keeping the pool room and the store from burning down. The efforts of the Cozy Corner customers did save the store and the pool room, but the only sure-enough professionally staffed whorehouse there ever was in Mayberry was soon just a pile of charred wood, ashes, and memories, all accompanied by a drifting haze of blue smoke. Zuby was greatly relieved when she saw that everyone, especially Doster, had escaped the burning building unharmed. Shortly after she saw that Doster had gotten out of the building safely, Zuby did run straight home and started fixin' supper.

When Doster finally came back home that evening and reported that there had been a fire at Cozy Corner, Zuby reacted with feigned surprise and concern. "Was anyone hurt in the fire? Did everything burn up?" She was just full of questions.

Doster didn't think anyone was hurt, but he did know that at least one of the buildings had burned plumb to the ground. "That's a real shame," commented Zuby, "but your supper is getting cold."

Rumors about Cozy Corner continued to be a major topic of gossip around Mayberry for years after it was gone. Some folks who had seen Zuby near Building Number Three suspected that she might have been connected to the fire, but no one ever made any outright accusations.

Building number three was never rebuilt, and it wasn't but just a couple more years until the dam was finished and most all of Ed's business went away. He closed the pool room down in 1939, and the store was closed down the year after that, making Cozy Corner just a couple of rickety old buildings with interesting histories.

As many Mayberry folks as I have asked, no one ever could or would tell me if there was ever any of the local talent employed to work at the Cozy Corner Building Number Three. My guess is that most all of the employees of the "Private Club" were brought in from Danville or even a ways farther off from some other place.

Doster seemed to improve his behavior after that fire though. Zuby must have forgiven him, and it may be that Doster never knew anything about what she actually knew. The best part of the story though, is about how Doster and Zuby, along with their whole passel of grown-up children, happily celebrated their golden wedding anniversary in June of nineteen and eighty-two.

Once, during prohibition, I was forced to live for days on nothing but food and water.

W.C. Fields

Hangin' Around

From the nineteen thirties on into the nineteen seventies, the Mayberry Store, was operated by Coy Yeatts. Coy was a rather serious fellow, very conservative in many ways, and someone who had no use for alcoholic beverages in any form. But Mr. Coy, as he was often called, was a business man who was trying to make a living at a time when most of the folks in Mayberry simply didn't have a lot of money. He needed to keep every customer the store had, so he decided that as long as there was no disturbance, no public display of alcohol, and no loud, vulgar, or profane language, he would just not take notice if some of his customers slipped around behind the back of the store every now and then to take a nip of the booze they had hidden back there.

Like just about every country store in America in the early part of the past century, the Mayberry Store had its cohort of loafers. There was a number of regulars who either loafed around the store most of the time it was open, or could at least be depended upon to make regular appearances there several time a week.

In the nineteen forties and fifties, the customer who kept the most regular hours at the Mayberry store was probably John, an older fellow who lived just over the hill and spent most of his waking hours – and quite a few of his sleeping ones – at the Mayberry Store. John had been a really hard worker when he was a younger man, but now that he was mostly retired, he spent much of the regular work week and most all of his Saturdays just loafing around the store, gossiping, playing checkers and occasionally snoozing. He spent so much of his time at the store that his sister Jettie, who cooked and kept house for him, would occasionally come into the store to buy a few essentials and see if her brother was still among the living.

One of the things that made John readily recognizable was his constantly disheveled state of dress. One might have mistaken John for a street person, had there been such a thing in Mayberry. He always wore many layers of rumpled clothing and the shoestrings of the oversized brogans he always wore were never tied.

In his later years, John seemed to have reserved what little energy he had for making moonshine. He was generally known as Mayberry's most dependable source of booze, but the quality of the stuff he supplied was rather erratic. Depending on whom you asked, John was either the maker of some "pretty good stuff," or he was accused of making "the godawfullest stuff that anybody ever tried to drink." It is possible that those could just have been different peoples' reactions to what was essentially the same product, but most people thought that the stuff that he personally made was pretty good. Sometimes, though, he just got tired of making it himself and would sell hooch that had been made by another local moonshiner who was somewhat less skillful.

John's reputation as reliable 'shiner suffered some serious damage for a time when a fellow who sometimes helped out around his still let it be known that John had found a dead opossum floating in one of his mash boxes. He said that John had just shoveled the dead critter out of the mash and run the wash through the still anyway. When asked about the incident, John declared that the possum wasn't actually dead. "He was just passed out," according to John. "It looked like he must have drunk it least two or three gallons of the wash."

It was well known around Mayberry that John had a small still located somewhere up off of Old Wagon Road, and the revenuers would probably have had little difficulty locating it, had they been so inclined. But the State ABC Agents were not all that interested in small time operators such as John. They really did not consider it worth their time and effort to try to find a piddling little still that someone like John would set up just to make a little 'shine for himself and his friends. The moonshiners that the State and Federal Agents were mostly interested in were large-scale producers. As long as nobody was being poisoned by any of the small-timers, the state and federal agents concentrated on the larger operations and left stills such as John's for the county law enforcement to deal with. Local law enforcement was usually occupied with matters more pressing than shutting down small-time part-time moonshiners such as John.

Over the last few years, the sheriff and his deputies had found and chopped up John's still a couple of times, but John had always been forewarned of the raid. Not only was he nowhere near the still when the raids had occurred, but the most valuable parts, the copper boiler cap and the worm, had been removed and hidden away by the time the officers arrived. One day, however, communications broke down and the sheriff and a couple of deputies were able to surprise John just as he was finishing up a run. The officers gave the Commonwealth's Attorney a sworn deposition that they had observed John in the actual process of filling jars with illegal spirits and arranging them in a case of similar jars. John later described his ordeal to the folks at the store. "When that-there Sheriff stepped out of the bushes and hollered out that I was under arrest," John lamented, "the onlyiest thing I could think to do was just to hold my breath 'til I died."

The officers placed John under arrest and then took him to the county seat for arraignment. Of course, John did not have the $100 he needed for bail, but he was allowed to call the Mayberry Store and ask if there was anyone there who would come bail him out. He also asked for someone to please get word to his sister Jettie, so that she would not be worried about him, should he have to stay locked up in the county jail while he awaited trial.

Coy Yeatts answered the telephone when John's call came in, and he assured John that he would get word to Jettie about John's situation as soon as possible. That did not take long at all, because right after Coy had hung up the phone, Jettie walked into the store looking for her brother.

When Coy told Jettie that John had been arrested and jailed and that he needed a hundred dollars for bond, she was less than sympathetic. "I don't have no hunnert dollars," she declared, "and if I had a hundred dollars, I wouldn't use it to bail out John." After thinking about it for a while though, she had a change of heart. "I do feel sorry for John, sittin' down there in that ol' jail," she told the folks at the store, "but I really ain't got no hundred dollars." Then she cheerfully added, "Well, at least now maybe he'll have enough time to keep his dang shoes tied."

In addition to its manyother functions, the Mayberry Store also served as the community dispensary. The local medical practitioner, Dr. Dave Robertson had passed away a few years before, and there was now a twenty mile distance between Mayberry and the nearest doctor. That meant that for all but really serious complaints, most Mayberry residents doctored themselves. There were several shelves in the Mayberry store that were dedicated to patent medicines and cure-alls, and Coy Yeatts was always willing to stock the latest non-prescription nostrums that salesmen would bring by. The salesmen would often leave a supply of brochures that described how sufferers could best benefit from the products' curative powers.

Among the many non-prescription medications that could be found on the shelves at the Mayberry Store were both Peruna (about twenty-five percent alcohol) and Paregoric (four percent opium), either of which was absolutely guaranteed to make the complainant feel better, at least for a little while. Since Coy Yeatts seemed to remember everything the salesmen would tell him about what each of the medicines were for and how they should be administered, a lot of folks began coming to him for advice on how to treat their everyday aches and pains.

Lloyd, who often worked at helping John run his moonshine still, was usually happy to take payment for his work in the form of the product of their labor. On any Saturday afternoon, it was a common sight to see Lloyd staggering down the Mayberry Road toward the store, soused to the gills. He never caused any trouble around the store though. He would just buy himself a Moon Pie and a bottle of pop, and then find some place to sit where he was out of everyone's way and he could just sit and listen. Most of the time, his presence at the store was hardly noticed.

One Saturday afternoon, however, when Lloyd

staggered into the store, he was looking mighty peaked. He walked over and propped himself up against the counter, rubbed his stomach and asked, "Mr. Coy, you got anything for a bellyache? My belly's hurtin' me somethin' terrible! Its been hurtin' me terrible all day!

Although Coy figured that Lloyd's problem was likely to have been caused by some of the stuff he had been drinking, he was sympathetic to Lloyd's complaint just the same. He occasionally suffered digestive difficulties of his own, and the store had begun stocking a new medication that he had found to be quite helpful. It was mostly being promoted as a cure for what was had begun to be called *acid indigestion*, and several of the folks at the store had tried out the new medicine. Everyone who had used it declared that Alka-Seltzer was especially good for a bellyache.

Nowadays, Alka-Seltzer comes in foil packets, but back then the big white tablets came stacked inside large glass tubes with screw-on tops. The store was stocked with both the short tubes containing eight tablets for a quarter, and the tall economy-size tubes of twenty tablets that sold for fifty cents. Coy Yeatts handed Lloyd a small tube that had already been opened, but which still contained several of the quarter-sized white tablets. "Here," he told Lloyd, "why don't you try a couple of these? They're supposed to work real good for a belly ache." No one thought to tell Lloyd that the tablets were supposed to be taken by drinking them after they had been dissolved in a glass of water.

Lloyd gratefully accepted the tube of tablets, then weaved his way over to the refrigerator and extracted a bottle of 7-Up soda. As he pried the cap off his bottle, everyone in the store was kind of watching and wondering what he was going to do next, and Lloyd did not disappoint them. Tucking his drink into the crook of his arm, Lloyd screwed the top off of the tube of Alka-Seltzer and shook three or four of the tablets out into his palm. Then, before anyone could advise him to the contrary, he popped all of them into his mouth at once.

The customers were all staring at Lloyd, not quite believing what he was doing, but no one made a move to stop him. Lloyd chomped down on the tablets a few times and after unsuccessfully trying to swallow them dry, he washed them down by chugging his 7-Up.

Lloyd just stood there for a couple of minutes, bracing himself against the refrigerator, as his eyes began bugging out. His eyes were opening wider and wider and he was rubbing his tummy, as he staggered toward the front of the store. Up front, he thumped down the empty 7-up bottle and propped up against the counter as he searched in his pockets for the money to pay for his drink. As he plopped down his dime, Lloyd shook his head and patted himself on the stomach again. “Oh Lordy-mercy-me,” he declared. “Them things sure are a-carryin’ on in there.”

As Lloyd wobbled out through the front door of the store, Coy called out after him, wanting to know if he was going to be all right. Lloyd stopped for a moment and turned, but after giving a couple of mighty belches, he declared himself to be just fine and continued on his way.

The very next Saturday, Lloyd was right back at the store, tanked as usual, but this time he was proclaiming his own sincere testimonial regarding the miraculous curative powers of *Alka-Seltzer*.

Another of regulars at the Mayberry Store was Harlow. He had been a rather tough character when he was young, even to the extent of pulling a couple of years of hard time for severely slicing up a fellow with whom he had a disagreement. That had happened years before, and as an older man he seemed to be mostly lazy and harmless, although he did continue to carry the reputation of someone who was not to be trifled with. Even with his prison record, he had been able to find work guarding convicts for the county for a time when there was a lot of highway construction in the area and good help had been hard to find. Some said that the Sheriff had hired him as a convict guard because he thought that Harlow would not hesitate to shoot any prisoner who might try to escape. At least that was the message that the Sheriff had spread among the convicts on the county road gang that Harlow was guarding.

A family affliction of hereditary glaucoma began to destroy Harlow's eyesight when he was still a fairly young man, and that ended his potential for most employment. He attended the state school for the blind for a brief time, where he learned some manual crafts such as making dippers from coconut hulls and assembling leather belts and purses. The crafts he made were sold in the Mayberry store, but their sale really did not generate much income, and it was really for the best that he did not have a family to support.

Even with his impaired vision Harlow was somehow able to negotiate the half-mile shortcut from his home to the Mayberry Store, even though the path meandered across open fields and through patches of woods and required crossing a creek and climbing over several fences. Some of the other loafers alleged that Harlow could see pretty much of everything he wanted to see.

Harlow spent a lot of time sitting outside at the front of the store, usually in a place where the sunlight was bright enough that he could see well enough to whittle. It may have been that he liked to whittle out front as a way of displaying his large ornate lock-blade knife, a weapon which might also remind folks around the store that he was a man with a past.

He would often take a cane bottomed chair out from inside the store and sit outside, with the chair tipped back against the store front. He always wore a light-colored wide-brimmed western style hat pulled down over his forehead, possibly to obscure the fact that the cornea of his eyes had become clouded. Harlow bothered no one, rarely made a purchase, and only carried on sparse conversations. He would, however, frequently engage other loafers in a game or two of checkers, a diversion at which Harlow truly excelled. In the summer when the days were long and the weather was nice, Harlow must have put in many a full forty-hour week at that store.

Sometimes, Harlow would get up and kind of feel his way around the side of the store, on around to the back of the store and into a thicket of rhododendron next to the small creek that ran past the building. The thicket was the location of the hidey-hole where he kept his jar of moonshine. No one ever dared to bother Harlow's liquor, even though he always hid it in the same place and he never seemed to have any difficulty in locating the jar himself. It eventually became clear to everyone that there was often something in addition to his impaired vision that made it difficult for Harlow to negotiate the terrain around the store.

When Richard would show up at the store, he would often be driving his dad's car. Although he did not yet have his driver's license, his dad would sometimes allow him to drive the family car for short excursions around Mayberry. These would just be short trips such as the half mile from their home near Mayberry Creek to the Mayberry Store or over to their farm called the Moore Place. Sometimes, without telling his dad, he would even drive down the Lower Dam Road to the pinnacle overlook.

Folks who restricted their driving to within a few miles of Mayberry and avoided driving on the Blue Ridge Parkway had little chance of ever encountering a law-enforcement officer. Mayberry folks understood the situation was so well that a lot of them just never bothered to get their driver's licenses in the first place.

For as far back as I can remember, Richard's dad always seemed to have had the nicest, newest cars of anyone we knew. But when his dad – my Uncle Neil – got that new nineteen and fifty-two DeSoto two-door hardtop with the "Firedome V-8" engine, he had a car that was really over the top. It was the sleekest, fanciest, most gussied up automobile anyone in Mayberry had ever seen.

Richard and several other of our cousins were at our grandparents' home on a Saturday afternoon one summer, when we were all surprised by Uncle Neil granting permission for Richard to drive a bunch of us the short distance from Grandpa's house up the Mayberry Road to the store. We all knew the reason Richard wanted to drive to the store was that he really wanted to show off his Dad's new car, but we were all cool with that. We were just excited to have the opportunity to take a little ride in such a fancy automobile. We were also pretty sure that Richard would fudge on his Dad's permission and drive on up to turn around at the Mayberry Church and then ease back down the road to the store. We were all just happy to be treated to as much riding in that snazzy new car as we could get.

Richard drove the long route, just as we expected, going past the store and turning around at the church before driving back and parking the big car in the narrow space between the road and the loafer's bench in front of the store. It was a typical Saturday afternoon, with a lot of the Mayberry loafers hanging around. As was also typical of a Saturday afternoon, some of the folks out front had obviously had imbibed more than just a nip of two of some locally produced schnapps. Everyone knew that those guys were allowed to sit on the bench out front, periodically going around in back of the store to take their nips from the jar. This would sometimes continue until some of them were practically crawling, but that was okay, just so long as there was no disturbance.

We just sat there, reared back on the fat leather seats inside of the car as it was parked in front of the store, just waiting for the customers to take notice of the new DeSoto. After a while, a couple of the more energetic guys got up and walked over to the car and ambled around it, scrutinizing, admiring, and commenting on the vehicle.

In 1952, there were not all that many options available on a car, even an up-scale model like that DeSoto. That car had just about every original equipment accessory that could be ordered. It had a radio and a heater, of course, and it also had turn signals, a feature that was still an option back then. It had also come equipped with white-wall tires, mud flaps, side mounted rear-view mirrors, fog lights, and two-tone paint. Most impressive of all, there were no roof pillars between the front and rear windows of the car! For some reason, now lost in history, the absence of the roof pillars was what caused a car to be designated as a "hard-top,"

This DeSoto car was also equipped with an option that I can recall seeing on only one or two other automobiles. The support for the outside rear-view mirror mounted on the driver's door housed two small gauges – one of them a *thermometer* and the other an *altimeter*. It was a safe bet that no one in Mayberry had ever seen a car tricked up with something like that before.

One of the more interested onlookers was Lee, one of the Mayberry residents who typically would spend his Saturday afternoons hanging around the store. Today, like most Saturdays, Lee appeared to be have been nipping rather heavily at the fruit jar. He stumbled over to the car, then weaved around it two or three times, carefully scrutinizing it from top to bottom. Eventually, he approached the driver's window, expecting that Richard would fill him in on all of the details.

"Mighty nice car you got there, Richie," he addressed our cousin in the driver's seat. "I rekon it's your dad's."

"Thanks. Yeah, it is Dad's car, but I get to drive it a lot," Richard fibbed.

"Boy, hit's got 'bout ever thing they is on it, I rekon. White walls, radio, two-tone…," he walked around the car again, admiringly ticking off the features, one-by-one. But as he came back around to the driver's window he adopted a puzzled expression. He had just noticed the two gauges built in with the rear view mirror. "What's all that for?" he asked, pointing to the gauges.

Richard was more than happy to demonstrate his technological sophistication. “Well, this one here’s a thermometer,” he explained, pointing to one of the gauges, “and that other one there is an altimeter.”

“Al-ti-me-ter?” queried Lee. “I ain’t never heard of that. What’s uh al-ti-me-ter for?”

“An altimeter is a gadget that tells how high you are,” Richard innocently explained.

“You kiddin’ me,” responded Lee. “Boy, I could sure use one o’ them things.”

Lee then bent over toward the gauge until his face was just inches away. “Whew, whew, whoooo,” he puffed onto the face of the altimeter gauge. “How high does it say that I am?” he wanted to know.

Just a few people had shuttled in and out of the Mayberry Store on that cold, foggy, drizzly Saturday afternoon, but Babe and Willie were two of the regulars who had been there the whole afternoon, just sitting in the back and staying close behind the warm stove. They both had been sipping regularly from Willie’s flask of brandy, just drinking out of boredom. After a while, babe stood up and walked around behind the counter, then reached up and hooked his finger into the loop of twine that held the battered old fiddle and lifted it from the nail. He then he lifted the bow from off of its own nail, and carried the fiddle and bow back to where he had been seated.

Babe plucked each string in turn, making the few adjustments of the pegs that were required to bring the fiddle into tune. Then he commenced to saw a soft, mournful melody. Babe's playing soon prompted Willie to get up and grasp the neck of the guitar that was lying on the counter behind him. He lifted the guitar and took a seat facing Babe, and with a few plucks on the strings and twisting of the tuning machines he brought the guitar into almost being in tune with the fiddle. Willie began to strum the strings with his thumb, softly following whatever tune it may have been that Babe was playing.

Babe settled in on the Charlie Poole song, *Never Let Your Deal Go Down*, and as he sang a couple of verses, Willie hummed along in harmony. That led Babe into playing *Lay My Head Beneath the Rose*, a Carter Family song that they both knew well enough to sing a couple of verses together. Willie harmonized mournfully with Babe lead as they sang…

Darlin' I am growing old.
Soon I'll lay in sweet repose.
When I'm gone, I ask a favor.
Lay my head beneath the rose.

The combination of the dreary day, the sad song, and the booze they had consumed really began to get to the two besotted old pals.

As Babe paused from his fiddling to take a nip, Willie spoke up, his eyes misty with tears. "You know Babe, I really love that song," he blubbered. "When I die, I want you and the Shelor Boys to play that song at my funeral."

"I hope I never live to see that day, Willie," Babe sincerely assured his old friend.

"Well, I hope I don't either, Babe," Willie solemnly agreed.

If there was ever any commerce in moonshine that took place anywhere around the Mayberry Store, it never directly involved either the store or the proprietor. There was doubtlessly some moonshine trade that did take place among the customers, but that always took place in the laurel bushes back behind the store and out of sight of the owner. On the other hand, there were a couple of other stores that were not too far from Mayberry and that usually did stock a little moonshine for their special customers.

One of the people who made much of the booze stocked by stores that did sell moonshine was a fellow who had just kind of showed up in the community one fine day, telling. folks that his name was, believe it or not, Thomas Jefferson. After he got to know some of the local folks a better, he told them about how he had been a hobo for most of his life and then sometimes share tales about his many travels through California and all over the West. Somewhere in those travels, he had apparently learned a thing or two about making moonshine.

Although "Tom Jeff," as he was known, had come there from no one knew where, he perfectly fit the stereotype of a mountain moonshiner. He was tall and lanky, sported a long black beard, and he always wore bibbed overalls and a battered felt hat. He was especially known for his successful strategy of evading the "revenooers" by frequently moving his still from one location to another, but his only means of transporting it was hauling it in his big old steel-wheeled wheelbarrow. Sometimes, he could be heard moving his still at night, with the boiler, the cap, the coil, and the thumping keg all piled into the wheelbarrow and all of those parts rattling and clanking as he rolled them down the middle of the Blue Ridge Parkway. The fact that the still was being moved was not a secret locally, since folks who lived half a mile away could hear the racket as he rolled it past.

Tom Jeff had some creative ways of distributing his product, and one of his favorites involved the use of a hollow stump that was located right beside the Blue Ridge Parkway. Those who knew the location and wanted to buy moonshine would just put three dollars in the hollow stump, then come back the next day and find a pint of white liquor in place of the money, compliments of Thomas Jefferson.

A friend I grew up with told me about being in a local general store one day when Tom Jeff rolled his old wheelbarrow up and left it sitting right in front of the store. Although the cargo in the wheelbarrow was concealed by an old tarp, everyone at the store assumed it was moonshine, since they could hear the glass jars clinking together as he rolled up. Tom Jeff came into the store, and while he was conducting his business with the owner, a sheriff's deputy pulled his car up to the front of the store and right beside the wheelbarrow. The deputy stepped out of his car, not five feet from the wheelbarrow load of booze and walked right past it and into the store. The deputy made a small purchase, chatted amicably with Tom Jeff and the store clerk for a few minutes, and left, totally unaware that he had been parked just a few feet from a wheelbarrow load of white lighting.

Occasionally, folks traveling along back paths in the area would encounter Tom Jeff lying along the trail, apparently incapacitated from too much testing of his own product. Oddly though, whenever he was found in that condition, either passed out or asleep, he always had one of his eyes wide open. Some said that it was because he had a glass eye that was never closed, while others claimed that he always slept with one eye open, just so he could keep one eye on his moonshine.

The friend who told me about the wheelbarrow load of booze also told me about an encounter he had with Tom Jeff one cold, bright, moonlit night. He was just a young kid at the time, but he had stayed late at the nearby general store, unworried about having to walk back home because it was such a bright night.

He was running along a narrow trail that was a shortcut back to his home when he saw something blocking the path and heard it making a strange noise. "Could that be a bear? A wild boar?" he worried, as he cautiously approached.

The youngster soon realized that it was only Tom Jeff lying there across the trail, sound asleep and snoring. He had his head propped up against a stump on one side of the path and his feet propped up on a log on the other side. Tom Jeff woke up as the boy approached, but he kept on gazing up at the sky.

"Have a seat son," he advised the boy. "Put yer feet up on this log here and warm 'em up by the light of that big ol' moon up there."

I always carry a flask of booze in case of snakebite. I also carry a small snake. W.C. Fields

Snake Bite Medicine

The list of weasel words that are used to refer to illicit alcoholic beverages is practically endless. Depending on the location and the situation, spirits of dubious provenance may be referred to as firewater, old red-eye, rotgut, hooch, booze, corn squeezins, mountain dew, white lightning, moonshine, 'shine, John Barleycorn, who-shot-John, alligatorpis, old pop-skull, blind pig, spiritus frumenti, bath tub gin, alcamahol, schnapps, rheumatism medicine, and the list goes on and on. I have known more than one person who consumed ardent spirits in significant quantity but who would refer to them using some of the most creative labels you can imagine. It was simply required that the labels not contain any identifying words such as *liquor* or *whisky*.

My personal favorite among the many euphemisms by which hard liquor is sometimes known is the term I would often hear used when I was a kid. A neighbor, someone who also happened to be an enthusiastic consumer of our locally produced spirits, would unfailingly refer to the illicit beverage he consumed using this one particular name. Whether he already had a quantity in his possession or was just thinking about how he could get his hands on some, he was usually concerned about maintaining the availability of what he called his *snake bite medicine*. I would sometimes hear other people refer to spirits, especially moonshine, using that same name, and to my mind, the name has always been especially apt and humorous. Even back then, I'm sure

I must have known that "snake bite medicine" was used as a euphemism for hard liquor because there were so many folks who kept a supply of it handy, under the pretext that it might be needed if someone in the household happened to get bitten by a venomous snake. In Marc Connelly's play from the 1930's, *The Green Pastures*, the author has Noah pleading with the Lord to allow him to take a large supply of snake bite medicine with him on the Ark, using the argument that, with all those venomous snakes on board, they should have plenty of booze, just in case he or his sons got bitten.

While some historians contend that the term *moonshine* has not always been the preferred term used among big-time producers in the South, it has always been the most common term used for illegal spirits that I have heard used. Here in the Blue Ridge Mountains, the other terms for illegal alcohol I would most commonly hear used *booze, hooch*, and of course, *snake bite medicine.*

Although the use of liquor as a traditional remedy to alleviate the effects of being bitten by a venomous snake is well documented, according to practitioners of modern medicine, drinking alcohol as a treatment for a venomous snake bite is not recommended. A drink of liquor following a venomous snake bite might relieve the pain somewhat, and possibly have some calming effect as a placebo, but physiologically, it is worse than no treatment at all. This is especially true if the bite was inflicted by a pit viper.

If you have the misfortune of being bitten by a venomous snake while in the Blue Ridge Mountains, it is almost a certainty that you will have been bitten by a pit viper. The only venomous snakes that habituate the Appalachian region of the country are the copperhead and a few different species of rattlesnake, all of which are pit vipers. The venom of all pit vipers is a blood coagulate, and according to what I read, one of the worst treatments one could possibly self-inflict after having been bitten by a pit viper would be the imbibing of alcohol. Alcohol increases the rate of blood circulation, and when one has just been injected with snake venom, an increase in the rate at which the venom is distributed through the body is the last thing one would want,.

The original purpose of this essay was not to provide the reader with advice on how to treat snake bites, so I will have no more to say about that except to add that I have read that here in the United States, in approximately sixty percent of the cases where a human is bitten by a venomous snake, some consumption of alcohol (by the human of course) is involved. The author of the article in which that statistic appeared, however, was adamant that the statistic applies in only those cases in which the alcohol was drunk by the victim *before* the bite was inflicted.

Note: The classification of copperheads, rattlesnakes, and cottonmouth moccasins together as pit vipers is because of the infrared sensing organs with which all of these species of snake are equipped. The pits are located just below and in front of their eyes, and although you may not wish to get close enough to identify a viper by its pits, it is one means of positive identification. The heat sensing organs within the vipers' pits serve as their guidance system as they strike, which explains why loose jeans are considered to be among the best defenses against being bitten by a venomous snake.

Although the original purpose of this essay was to provide an explanation of why alcoholic beverages are sometimes referred to as "snake bite medicine," now that I have begun talking about snakes, I cannot help but to continue. This, in itself, is a tendency that has a long and storied history.

Like so many folks, I seem to have retained much of the fact and fiction about snakes and their interaction with humans that I have been hearing for most of my life. I think I began mentally cataloging snake lore years ago, when I began to notice that anytime a brief period of silence might occur among a group of friends or kinfolk, the very mention of the word *snake* would invariably revive the conversation. Even today, in any sort of congenial gathering, all anyone has to do is to make a statement – any brief comment or observation that includes the word *snake* – and once the magic word has been uttered, there is almost a guarantee that a lively discussion will begin, usually a discussion in which everyone present wishes to participate.

There are many reasons why people are fascinated by snake lore, but the most basic reason is probably that most people harbor a greater or lesser degree of fear and loathing toward snakes. Although some of us may suppress it better than others, those emotions are always there, right under the surface, just waiting to be released in the event of any reptilian encounter. It is likely that we have those responses because of the way we were taught from the cradle that snakes are creatures to be feared, and how we learned from Genesis that the serpent is the epitome of evil.

One problem most of us have with snakes is that we are usually unaware of them until there is less distance between ourselves and the snake than we would prefer. In an encounter with a snake, there is often insufficient time and space for us to make a thoughtful assessment of whether the snake presents any actual threat. Some of us may have learned to react more or less rationally in an encounter with a snake, but for many people, a conscious suppression of their natural revulsion is required to maintain a calm facade.

It may be that many people simply cannot help the way they react when they find themselves in the presence of a snake. No matter how small or harmless the reptile may be, more often than not, a human/snake encounter ends with the snake being pounded into a bloody morass. Many people feel no guilt whatsoever after pulverizing any snake, even if it is obvious that the snake is of a harmless variety. A common rationalization heard from those who have the reflex response of destroying any snake on sight is some version of “so far as I am concerned, all snakes are poisonous.” Many people who are consistently kind and caring for most creatures great and small are often found to harbor an aversion toward snakes. These are normally good people who truly possess a deep and abiding affection for all of God’s creatures, with the exception of snakes.

A common response from people who might feel some tinge of guilt after having dispatched a harmless, non-threatening serpent is to convince themselves and those nearby that (a) the snake was indeed of a venomous species, and that (b) it definitely presented a clear and present danger to them and/or their loved ones.

Just as there are definable characteristics associated with each of the many different species of snake, there are certain definable characteristics associated with each of the many genre of snake tales. In stories involving water snakes, for example, the reptiles involved are almost always referred to as being "water moccasins." Although there are many varieties of non-venomous water snakes here in the South, the term *water moccasin* is almost always used to imply that the snake being referred to is a venomous cottonmouth water moccasin. Unfortunately for many of the non-venomous species of water snake, many of them do indeed have patterns of coloration that bear some resemblance to that of the venomous cottonmouth. This, of course, means that cottonmouth moccasins and non-venomous species of water snake experience similar mortality rates in their interactions with humans.

One of the most frightful – and therefore long-lived – Southern snake legends is the one about the kids who allegedly went swimming in a farm pond and encountered a nest of cottonmouth moccasins on the bottom. In the many permutations of the tale, one or more of the kids are struck by the cottonmouths, with the claim being made that the unfortunate children were bitten anywhere from tens to hundreds of times and therefore quickly perished. While there doubtlessly has been an incident somewhere sometime in which someone swimming in a pond encountered a cottonmouth in the water and was possibly even bitten, there are a number of problems with the legend as it is usually recited. While cottonmouth moccasins do sometimes swim in water, they live near the water rather than in it. Being air breathing creatures, they do not nest underwater and they can swim underwater for only short periods of time.

One way to distinguish between any venomous and nonvenomous snakes you may see swimming in the water is by the extent to which the snakes are submerged. Pit vipers have less dense bodies than most non-venomous species of snake and therefore tend to swim more on top of the water rather than through it.

I use the general term *pit viper* here because, in addition to cottonmouth moccasins, copperheads and most species of rattlesnake can also swim quite well. But you didn't really want to know about that, did you?

Anyway, one is not likely to win friends by telling someone that the snake tale he has just told you has little probability of being true. Most tellers of suspect snake stories can provide you with a provenance such as how their daddy knew someone who knew the family who owned the farm on which the tragedy occurred.

In the Piedmont regions of North Carolina and Virginia, the venomous snake most commonly encountered by far is the copperhead. It is therefore understandable that unless a snake has a definitive pattern or coloration – being shiny black or longitudinally striped, for instance – creating an appearance that makes it almost impossible to not be identified as being nonvenomous, it will often automatically be assumed to be a copperhead. Some people do find it hard to suppress their imaginations.

Some years ago I encountered a young boy in our neighborhood as he walked up and down our street, proudly displaying a snake he had just killed. The snake was totally black except for the white ring around its neck and a patch of white on the back of its head. Although that coloration, along with its slender body, unambiguously showed it to be a beneficial king snake, the kid was proudly proclaiming the details about how he had just dispatched a deadly copperhead to any who would listen.

While growing up in the Appalachians, even though I

was continually exposed to stories regarding the plethora of deadly serpents with which the mountains were supposedly infested, I concluded at a rather young age that the hoop snake was definitely a mythical creature. In case you have not previously been warned about the deadly hoop snake, it is supposedly a particularly aggressive and highly venomous serpent that pursues it victims by grasping its tail in its mouth and rolling after them, like an (ahem) hoop. They are quite speedy, I was told, and practically impossible to outrun in a downhill retreat. One thing that I did learn from the hoop snake myth is that some folks really do take their snake tales quite seriously. In elementary school, I was given a thorough thumping by an older boy who was seriously offended when I expressed my doubts regarding the veracity of his tales of terror involving his personal encounters with hoop snakes.

Being something of an outdoors person, I have made a serious effort to learn about snakes, especially wanting to know where I am most likely to encounter them and how to identify (and avoid) certain species. I would like to think such knowledge would allow me to react rationally when I do encounter a snake, and that is usually the case, provided I become aware of the reptile while we are still separated by a reasonable distance such as ten or more feet. Even after years of seeking to expand my knowledge about snakes, however, I still jump out of my skin if I happen to step on a garden hose that is hidden in tall grass.

I grew up in the Eastern Appalachians at an elevation sufficient to make encounters with venomous snakes relatively uncommon. Copperheads and rattlesnakes are encountered only occasionally in the region, and cotton mouth moccasins and coral snakes do not live there. But I soon learned that it was unwise to inform anyone that the "copperhead" they had just dispatched was actually a harmless corn snake or a beneficial hog-nosed snake.

If you should unexpectedly encounter a snake that is occupying your hanging basket or relaxing on top of the back door frame of your house, it is likely to be either a harmless common black snake or a gray rat snake. Both are beneficial and non-venomous to be sure, but can a snake accurately be described as harmless if it causes you to have a heart attack?

Not everyone is as fearless as my grandmother Mac, a resilient woman who continued to lived alone in a large ancient farmhouse well into her eighties. She did worry about falling, so she would often send me or another grandchild up to the attic when she needed to store or retrieve something. She would always send us up with an admonition to "not bother her pet blacksnake." She did indeed have a very large snake living in the attic. It was actually a gray rat snake, and it was probably over six feet in length. She would sometimes remark that she had rather have snakes living in her attic than have rats and mice in the house, and her pet snake did apparently limit her rodent problems.

I will have to admit that there are some ridiculous sounding snake tales that are actually true, and here is one that I personally know about. A sportsman acquaintance of mine was fishing on the Cape Fear River in eastern North Carolina, when a large snake dropped from an overhanging limb and into the bottom of his boat. Being a manly guy who never goes fishing unarmed, he fired his .357 magnum revolver at the snake six times, each shot making a hole through the bottom of his expensive Boston Whaler fishing boat. I tried to explain to my friend that a snake that is hanging out on a limb that is high over the water is probably one of a harmless variety of water snake. The heavy-bodied cottonmouth moccasins are not prone to climb very high up into trees, but he is still convinced that the snake that dropped into his boat was a cottonmouth. Fortunately or unfortunately, the snake somehow escaped the volley of bullets and slithered over the gunwale and into the water, so my friend was unable to confirm his conviction that he is the survivor of a narrow brush with death.

It is my philosophy that folks should spend their time worrying about hazards they may encounter in a direct proportion to which those hazards actually exist. It is therefore important to realize that here in the United States, one is about a hundred times more likely to succumb from being stung by some kind of wasp than from being bitten by a venomous snake. According to the government statistic I found on line, in the years from 2010 through 2014, there were twenty-three people in the country who were officially determined to have died as the result of a venomous snake bite. Three of the unfortunate souls who perished were Pentecostal snake handlers who were bitten while participating in religious services and who did not seek medical treatment. It is fairly certain, however, that none of the unfortunate snake handlers had consumed any alcohol, either before or after being bitten.

It is just a coincidence that in the process of writing this essay, I learned that in the past year there were sixty venomous snake bites reported in Mecklenburg County, North Carolina, the most heavily urbanized area of the state. It is believed that all of those bites were inflicted by Copperhead snakes, since that is the only venomous specie of snake known to live in that county. Fortunately, all of the victims recovered.

While I feel that I should apologize for getting so far afield from the subject, I might as well go ahead and mention that there is a significant distinction between creatures (such as snakes and scorpions) that are *venomous*, and things (such as chemicals and plants) that are *poisonous*.

As a means of making this distinction, just remember that if a snake is *venomous*, you will be harmed if *it* bites *you*. On the other hand, if a snake is just *poisonous*, you will only be harmed if *you* bite *it*.

It also might be useful to keep in mind that, while there are many species of creatures including snakes, insects, jelly fish, etc. that are venomous, in among the long list of things that are poisonous there are several species of mushroom and more than a few varieties of poorly made moonshine. It is also interesting to note that the toxins found in either poisonous mushrooms or poisonous moonshine are chemicals that attack the livers of humans who are unfortunate enough to ingest them. In the community where I grew up, I knew of five men who died as a result of drinking poisonous booze, but I know of none who perished from the bite of a venomous snake.

In defense of alcohol, I have done some really dumb things when I was sober too. Phil Harris

Beware of the Cat

Percy Whittaker pulled the heavy wooden door shut, then inserted his key into the lock and gave it a careful turn. After shaking the handle to make sure the door was locked, he withdrew the key, then carefully slipped that key off of his heavy ring of keys before clipping the key ring back onto his belt. Turning and taking a couple of quick steps away from the door, he swung his arm over his head, throwing the key over the road and into the piney woods, as far as he could send it. The time was two minutes after five o'clock p.m., the date was July 31, 1937, and the door of the United States Post Office in Beulah, Virginia, had been closed and locked for the last time.

As a Hoover supporting Republican, Percy Whittaker had known that his days of serving as the Beulah Postmaster were numbered from the day the country experienced the Democratic landslide that gave Roosevelt the Presidency. Percy was somewhat thankful that he had been able to hold on to his job for as long as he had. Some of the local politicians had lobbied hard to keep the Beulah Post Office open, and they were successful for a time. But southwestern Virginia was still stuck deep in the Great Depression, and the decision to close the Post Office had more to do with economics than with politics.

The post office at Meadows of Dan had been allowed to expand its rural free delivery service to include most of the areas once served by the Beulah Post Office, and most of the folks who used to pick up their mail in Beulah now had it delivered to mailboxes they had placed beside the roads near their homes. The number of post office box holders at the Beulah Post Office had dropped to less than twenty by the time Percy received the formal letter from the Postmaster General informing him that the post office would be closed at the end of the fiscal year. From that point, it was clear that no amount of political influence would save either the Beulah Post Office or Percy's job.

Even so, Percy would admit that life had treated him pretty well for the years he had served as postmaster. His salary may not have seemed like much by some standards, but when combined with the income from his farm-related activities, the Whittaker family had lived pretty well. Percy had managed to prosper throughout the depression, even with a wife and five kids to support, and he may have been one of the more well-to-do citizens of Beulah. It was a good deal while it lasted; Percy running the post office – not a very demanding task, really – while his wife kept house and the older children helped out on the farm.

Percy had hoped to get in at least twenty years of government service so he could retire with a full pension, but when it became clear that this would not happen, he began working on contingency plans. When it first began to look like the post office might be closed, he had applied for a job as timekeeper with the United States Department of the Interior. The government was starting the construction of the Blue Ridge Parkway through the area at that time, but the W.P.A. never seemed to have a position for someone with Percy's particular set of skills. He ended up spending much of his time during the last days of his postmaster's job concocting less conventional financial schemes.

After locking the post office door for the last time, Percy walked the half-mile to his house without once looking back or wondering if he had left anything important behind. As he turned to walk down the lane that led from the main road to his house, however, he felt a wave of disgust. He realized that now, just like everyone else, he would have to dig a hole in the shoulder the road and put in a post with a mailbox on top of it.

As soon as Percy got home, he went to the bed room, took off the bow tie and white shirt that had been his work-day uniform for the past fifteen years, and tossed them into in the bottom of the wardrobe. The next morning, instead of a white shirt and bow tie, Percy put on a blue chambray shirt, then stepped into a pair of bibbed overalls and pulled them up and onto his bony frame. After topping his angular face and thinning hair with a felt slouch hat, he looked at himself in the mirror, proudly observing that he now had the appearance of a classical mountaineer. This was a new day, and he was now dressed in what was to be his uniform for the remaining years of his life.

The Whittaker house sat about quarter of a mile off the main road, located on the back side of the eighty acres of bottomland that had been in the Whittaker family for generations. Half of that bottomland was usually planted in corn, and in late summer, the corn in that fertile field was often tall enough to obscure the view of the Whittaker house from the road. The home was accessed by a lane that turned off of the main road and ran along the upper side of the corn field before it turned down a gentle slope to an open area in front of the house. There was usually an old Model-A Ford parked beside the lane right in front of the house.

The lane continued on down past the house for a ways, passing the barn and the chicken lot, and finally ending at the bank of a rippling little branch known as Stoney Creek. The creek began as a spring branch back in the woods a half mile or so behind the house. It flowed through woods and onto the Whittaker farm, where it defined the lower boundary of the property, all the way to the point where it disappeared into a culvert and flowed under the road.

The setting of the Whittaker home could be described as idyllic, nestled at the foot of a ridge that was covered with Virginia white pines. Looking out from the front porch of the house and across the corn field toward the road, the view was dominated by Turkey Knob, a steep wooded prominence that rose abruptly a short distance from the far side of the main road. The front of the house was dominated by a large double-decked front porch that was framed by two large maple trees. The white clapboards and green shutters on the front of the house were always kept neatly painted, but many of the less visible parts of the house were in need of some attention. Percy had been giving some thought to how he was going to fix the place up, now that he would have more free time. He had been assuring his wife for years that he was going to fix the dilapidated back porch, and he planned to do that real soon. But right now, he had more pressing concerns.

Percy had a business plan that was directly related to his cornfield and to the Potter Boys, a couple of friends from down in the Big Bend section. For several years now, a large part of Percy's annual corn crop had been bartered to the Potter Boys as raw material, ingredients that were occasionally traded for an infusion of the Potters' finished product. The product, of course, was the Potter Boys' moonshine liquor, locally known for its exceptionally high quality and amazing potency.

Percy didn't drink a whole lot, usually limiting his alcohol consumption to a couple of healthy snorts for relaxation on Saturday evenings, and then possibly a couple more short snorts in the company of friends on Sunday morning. The Potter boys would often stop by to make their exchanges with Percy on Sunday mornings, while Percy's wife and kids were away. His wife was a pillar of the Church, and she and the younger kids regularly attended both Sunday School and Preaching at the nearby Beulah Baptist Church.

Although she had to have been somewhat aware of her husband's moonshine related activities, Mrs. Whittaker rarely questioned Percy's indulgences or business practices. She may have been a proud member of both the tee-totaling Beulah Baptist Church and the Women's Christian Temperance Union, but she also enjoyed the comfortable life she and her family had been living the past few years. She would really have preferred to not have known everything about whatever it was that Percy was up to.

Most of the liquor Percy obtained in his bartering with the Potters was either given away or sold instead of being drunk by him. In recent months, several pints of moonshine had been used as a way of expressing his gratitude to some local politicians for their efforts on his behalf. The careful distribution of some of the Potter's moonshine had surely been a factor in the Beulah Post Office staying open for as long as it did. Some more of the fine product had been expended as a way of encouraging county law enforcement to concentrate on more important concerns than the Potter's moonshining operation. An unspoken agreement insured that the Potters would be given advance notice when a raid on their still was unavoidable. Percy might have also retailed a few pints himself, but he only sold the booze to his friends. Come to think of it though, Percy really didn't have all that many enemies.

It wasn't that far from Percy's place in Beulah to the location where the Potter Boy's moonshine operation was hidden down on the Big Bend, at least it wasn't far if you knew the shortcut across Turkey Knob. If you wanted to drive a car from Beulah to Big Bend by way of the main road, however, that would require driving almost all the way to Meadows of Dan and then doubling back on Big Bend Road, a trip of almost five miles along a winding and unpaved mountain trail. It took less time and attracted less attention for Percy to ride his mule the mile or so across Turkey Knob to Big Bend whenever he needed to communicate directly with the Potters.

The Potter Boys were born down on Big Bend, but they didn't grow up there. They had spent much of their lives living with their daddy in West Virginia, with all three of them eventually working in the coal mines. After the daddy got the black lung and had to quit working in the mines, that was when the family had moved back to their home place on the Big Bend.

Although the Potter Boys, Loy and Roy, each weighed in at about three hundred pounds, and even though their weight was matched by their physical strength, they were basically quiet and gentle people. While they may not have had a lot of formal schooling, they were good folks, hard workers, and they were honest too, in their own way. Had they known some other way of making a living in a place like Big Bend, they surely would have preferred that to working in an occupation where being apprehended by law enforcement or having their equipment busted up was not a constant concern. The brothers never understood why the government cared so much about the way that they earned their modest living anyway. They would really have preferred to have gone back to mining coal, hard and dangerous work though it was, but they had to stay close to home so they could look after their ailing daddy.

The Potters all lived in their old farm house near Big Bend, where the family still owned a pretty good size piece of property. Their land ran all the way from the north side of Turkey Knob and all the way down to the river. Although it was of some considerable acreage, it was not of much value as farmland. The Potters had intended to run the farm when they moved back to Big Bend, but they soon found that their land on the rocky north slope of the mountain had been farmed out. They were able to run a few beef cattle there, but their corn growing never amounted to much.

The Potter Boys' daddy had a small pension, but the boys couldn't find much work close to home, at least nothing that paid anything like what they had made while they were working in the mines. They decided that the solution was to go into the business of making corn liquor, a trade that both their daddy and granddaddy had known quite well from way back. The Potters business plan hit a snag though, when they found they could not grow enough corn on their worn-out land to make their moonshining worthwhile. After they had gotten to know Percy Whittaker, however, things changed for the better. Percy was both a connoisseur of corn liquor and the owner of some highly productive bottom land, and he and the Potter boys soon settled on an arrangement that was to everyone's liking.

One of the first things Percy did after he and the Potters had gotten their new business arrangement going was to go to the Ford dealer over in Floyd and buy himself a brand-new shiny-black 1939 Ford V-8 coupe. Some of Percy's neighbors may have wondered if he had taken leave of his senses, but Percy didn't care. He had gotten a few dollars ahead, and he had been thinking about getting a new car for a long time. Now that it looked like he might be making some real money, he decided to get just what he wanted. Now he would have transportation other than his mule when his wife was out driving the Model A. He especially needed his own car while his wife and the kids were in church on Sundays. And if nothing else, the purchase of a new automobile could help the former postmaster overcome his feelings of diminished status within the community.

The precise model of Percy's new Ford was the *Deluxe Business Coupe.* That meant that the car came with the big new 221 cubic inch 85 horsepower flathead V8 engine and almost every option available at the time, including radio, heater, bumper guards, and mud flaps. Oddly enough, the Deluxe Business Coupe did not come with a rear seat. That was fine with Percy, because he did not need a back seat for his purposes, mostly tasks that did not include hauling the kids around. The Whittaker's old Model-A would still function well enough for Mrs. Whittaker drive to the store and haul the kids wherever they had to go.

Percy's new V8 Ford Coupe, not coincidentally, was the exact same make and model of automobile that was rapidly becoming the car most favored by the mountain boys who were hauling moonshine out of the Southern Appalachians at the time. The powerful V8 engine and the expansive trunk that could be extended all the way to the front seats made it the perfect moonshine hauler.

Percy's new car attracted so much attention that he decided "what the heck," and tried to live up to the image his car projected. Although he was actually a pretty awful driver, and he really had no plans to be hauling moonshine over any great distances or to ever try to outrun any law officers, he decided to try and create an image of himself as a daring mountain bootlegger. Percy paid out a tidy sum to a local mechanic who was expert in souping-up those Ford flathead engines, and that mechanic modified the engine of Percy's car to the extent that it was producing almost twice its original horsepower. Of course, the engine modifications reduced the car's gas mileage to a truly dismal figure, but that didn't bother Percy. The important thing was the way the engine would give such a magnificent rumble through its gutted mufflers and dual exhaust pipes in ordinary driving, and the ferocious roar it would emit whenever Percy romped on the accelerator. A '39 Ford Coupe with a hot engine like that was the penultimate status symbol among Percy's friends around Beulah, whether it actually served any useful purpose or not.

On warm and sunny Saturday afternoons, Percy could usually be found with his car parked down by the creek, washing it and lovingly applying another coat of wax to his new status symbol. Commercial car care products were hard to come by in Beulah in those days, but he had found that Johnson Floor Wax, the very same product that Mrs. Whittaker used to keep her floors so dangerously polished, also worked well on black Ford automobile paint. At least it worked well if one was willing to put in the elbow grease required to rub it on, rub it off, and then spend hours polishing the surface to a high gloss.

The Whittaker family's overweight and arrogant, long-haired raccoon tabby cat, Boomer, was also fond of Percy's new car. In fact, the warm hood of that new Ford Coupe quickly became Boomer T. Cat's favorite napping place. Boomer also developed a fondness for strolling through wet grass and then plodding through the dusty driveway before leaping up onto the hood of Percy's car. Once up on the shiny car hood, the cat found it necessary to parade up and down the hood a few times before settling down for his nap. One could always tell when the cat had paid a recent visit to the car, because of the way he would leave the hood thoroughly covered with a pattern paw prints surrounding the patch of long cat hair where he had been napping.

Just the idea that the spoiled cat dared to use the hood of Percy's prized possession as a place to perch and nap drove him to distraction. Sometimes, if he happened to catch Boomer napping on his car while the wife and the kids were not around, he would attempt to sneak up on the napping feline and douse him with a bucket of cold water, but the cat was usually too wary for that. Anytime Percy caught that cat sleeping on his car, however, Percy's minimal reaction would be to release string of profanity interspersed with threats of violence.

Guests who happened to be seated in the Whittaker parlor were sometimes startled when, right in the middle of a civilized conversation, Percy would jump from his chair and charge out of the front door and across the front porch.

Sometimes he would run out the door while shouting out a string of profane epithets describing the illegitimate pedigree of the cat, and such outbursts often culminated with Percy scooping up a clod of dirt from the drive and chucking it at the critter that had just been spied napping on the hood of his freshly waxed Ford.

Percy was obviously frustrated by the limited assortment of projectiles available to hurl at the cat, torn as he was between choosing a rock that might be effectively thrown, but which was likely to damage his car's finish, and a clump of sod that was less likely to harm the car, but was more difficult to throw effectively. Anyway, as soon as Boomer had been exiled to the far side of the creek, Percy would wipe off the hood, dust off his hands and walk back to the house, muttering to himself about the short life expectancy of the cat unless it underwent a change in its napping habits very soon. He would then return to the parlor and resume the conversation, even though he might be a little short of breath for a time. Other than continually glancing out the window to check on the status of his car, Percy would act as if nothing out of the ordinary had happened. Within a few minutes, however, Boomer would usually have returned to his favorite napping place.

If no visitors were around, Percy might also shout out gruesome descriptions of what he was going to do to that cat one of these days. Either blowing the cat to Kingdom Come with his shotgun or knocking him across the cornfield with a baseball bat were two of his most commonly vocalized fantasies. In spite of such threats, the cat knew well that he was perfectly safe. Boomer the Cat was beloved by every member of the family other than Percy, and besides, he would never take any action that might possibly inflict damage to his precious automobile. Still, "he'll think he's a Boomer when I get ahold of him," continued to be Percey's favorite comment regarding the uncertain future of the cat.

Prohibition may have come to an end five years earlier, but Percy had correctly judged that there would be little change in the demand for illegal booze in a dry community such as Beulah, where there was not an establishment that even sold beer. He had no intention of being just another hillbilly bootlegger, however. He and the Potter Boys were able to set up a sophisticated business arrangement with the owner of Beulah Mercantile Company, the large general store that was the economic center of the community.

Percy took on the roles of chief administrator, purchasing agent, salesman, and transportation manager of the new business. After the Potter Boys had finished doing all the hard work of making the moonshine, Percy would use his new business coupe to haul three or four cases of liquid corn from the Potter Boys' still near Big Bend up to back of Beulah Mercantile. At the rear of the Mercantile building, he would back up to the loading dock and raise the trunk lid of his car as though he was loading up his trunk with feed. Percy and an employee would then slip the moonshine into the back of the feed room, and the voluminous trunk of the Ford would then be loaded up with supplies such as sacks of sugar, canning jars, corn meal, and Milk Maker Dairy Feed. All of the supplies would be delivered to the Potter's still site, after Percy had made a couple of circuitous side trips, to confuse anyone who might be making note of his trips in and out of Big Bend.

It was known to many moonshiners across the country

that certain brands of feed for dairy cattle contained a fair percentage of malted grain, making them a product that could be used effectively in the manufacture of moonshine. Almost as cheap and faster fermenting than corn, its purchase did not attract the same attention that the buying large quantities of sugar and corn meal sometimes did. The moonshine formula that Percy and the Potter Boys had settled on involved the fermentation of a mixture of sprouted corn and corn meal from Percy' farm, plus the addition of Milk Maker Dairy Feed and sugar from the Mercantile. The exact proportions, of course, were a tightly guarded professional secret. Every week or so, a truck from Valley Milling Company would deliver a load of sugar and stock feed to Beulah Mercantile, and leave with several cases of corn liquor tucked away among sacks of grain and feed.

Within a year of Percy's retirement, production from the Potters' distillery had more than doubled, and while local law enforcement may have had some idea of what was going on, the judicious distribution of a few jars of corn squeezin's insured that there would be little problem from them. Unfortunately for the moonshiners, no such deals could be made with the Federal A.T.F. agents or the State Alcoholic Beverage Control Officers. They had recently become aware of an increase in the amount of moonshine coming out of the Beulah area, and they had decided that it was worthy of their attention.

Although Percy was indeed clever in his schemes, his participation in the moonshine business was made more difficult by his wife's lack of cooperation. Mrs. Whittaker, a heavily corseted woman with an adopted air of refinement, was imbued with Victorian values through and through. She had a low opinion of alcohol in general and of moonshining in particular. Her roots were from somewhere up the valley, so she thought of herself as being a member of the old Virginia aristocracy. She had even joined up with a lot of organizations such as the Daughters of the Confederacy, the Daughters of the American Revolution, the Order of The Eastern Star, and all that sort of thing. When Percy's downfall came, some folks thought it might have been Mrs. Whittaker who had tipped off the Federal agents, but that is doubtful. As a form of insurance, Percy had carefully pacified Mrs. Whittaker by making generous donations to the Beulah Baptist Church, donations made possible by the profits he was making in the new moonshining business.

In the late fall of 1939, however, Percy Whittaker achieved fame in a way no one could have ever imagined. Percy became the very first moonshiner in Virginia to be photographed by Federal Agents flying above, searching for stills from an airplane. The Government had now begun searching for illegal liquor operations through the use of aerial reconnaissance, and modern technology had now made it possible to take detailed photographs of anything below that was exposed. A candid photograph of Percy, taken from a low-flying airplane and blown up to half-page size not only appeared in the Roanoke Times, but it was also used as evidence in Percy's trial when it was held before a Federal judge in Abingdon.

The lawyer insisted that his client was a victim of mistaken identity, but in a very short trial, Percy was convicted on charges of conspiring to manufacture and transport illegal and untaxed spirits of alcohol.

Percy had been photographed while he was carrying a

case of moonshine through the woods, down the path from the still to his car. He had parked his car in a relatively open space, but even so, had there still been leaves on the trees, or had Percy not looked up at the airplane as it flew over him at a very low altitude, he may have not been identified. But no one who had ever seen Percy in person could have doubted that it was his protruding nose jutting skyward from under the slouch hat as it appeared in that picture. The photograph was so clear and sharp that the word "Mason" was readable on the top of the box he was carrying. The conclusive evidence however, was the photograph taken of Percy's Ford Coupe. The long trunk lid was fully raised, making the number on the black and white Virginia license tag as readable as a billboard to the camera in the airplane.

The defending lawyer also tried claiming that the box Percy was carrying was filled with canned peaches, but the Judge would have none of it. Why were there cases of canned peaches stacked in the middle of the woods, less than fifty yards from the site of an illegal still and several months after peach season? Also submitted as evidence was a photograph of several cases of mason jars stacked right by the still, and those cases appeared to be identical to the one Percy had been carrying when he was photographed. All of that evidence was totally damning.

As things turned out, Percy may have been kind of lucky. If he had been photographed while actually loading the cases into his car, the car could have been confiscated.

Percy earned the undying gratitude of the Potter Boys by claiming full responsibility for the entire moonshine operation and giving sworn testimony that he had built the still on their property without their knowledge. As a first-time offender and purported pillar of the community, he was sentenced to ninety days in jail, fined two-hundred dollars, and given three years of probation.

After spending just sixty days incarcerated near Lewisburg, Pennsylvania, Percy was released for good behavior. Rather than spending his time in contrition, however, Percy had apparently spent most of his time in the pokey carefully planning a new and improved moonshining operation. The Potter Boys were never charged with making moonshine, but their well-made, all-copper still was completely demolished by the Federal Agents, and it would take time and money to replace that. The family land on which the distillery was constructed could also have been confiscated if a connection to the Potters could have been proven. Percy's strategy in claiming responsibility for the distillery operation was to create leverage to get his business partners to help him set up a new, far more sophisticated, and much better hidden operation.

During his stint in prison, Percy decided that the location of his new distillery must be nowhere near the site of the former still. Of course, the Federal agents would now be keeping an eye on the Potter farm, and this new aerial reconnaissance business made it necessary to locate a still either in a building, in a cave, or at least in woods that were mostly pine. After he had been back home for a few months, Percy finally settled on what he considered to be the perfect location for a new moonshine operation, and he soon delivered that news to his former partners-in-crime.

On a Saturday afternoon, when Percy met with Loy and Roy Potter to tell them about the proposed location, he was prepared to convince them that they should help him start up the business again. He described the site he had selected as being easy to access, near an abundant source of clean water, and one that would be well concealed all year round. Best of all, it would be on land owned by the Federal Government, where no one would be in any danger of having their property confiscated. Instead of moving to a location that was even more remote and difficult to access, Percy reasoned, why not set the distillery up in a location convenient to both the raw materials and modern means of transportation. The place he had in mind was just a few hundred yards from his own back door, and the fact that it would be right under the noses of local law enforcement would be a benefit rather than a liability.

Stony Creek flowed onto Percy's property right after it made a sharp turn around the west end of Pine Ridge and before meandering southward along the lower edge of the field in front of the house. For the half-mile before the creek reached Percy's property, it ran across land that had recently been acquired by the National Park Service. Where it approached the Whittaker property, the branch had undercut the corner at the base of the ridge, creating an overhanging bank that was covered with large rhododendron, creating a sort of a living cave. The driveway to Percy's house could be used for access, there was nothing but rhododendron all along the creek, and there was nothing but a thick pine forest from the back of the house all the way to the foot of Pine Ridge and on up to the Parkway. The proposed location would be invisible all year long, summer and winter. The Potters were enthusiastic about the proposed location and it was agreed that construction of a new still under the overhang beside Stony Creek should begin right away. They decided they should get started the very next morning, while Mrs. Whittaker and the children were away at church.

When the Potter Boys arrived at the Whittaker home on Sunday morning, Percy met them out front. "You can drive your pickup down past the barn and into the woods," he told them. "You will be able to follow the creek to the end of Pine Ridge once we get it cleared out a little bit. For now, we can just walk around the house and through the woods." As he led them past the back of his house, he suggested, "It might be best if you boys don't walk over that rickety ol' back porch of ours."

Problems with the new still site began almost as soon as they started to work. The overhang was not sufficient to conceal the sort of operation Percy had in mind, and when they decided to dig out a cave to make provide more room, they found the back of the overhang to be solid flint rock. "Where there's a ridge, there's always a reason," philosophized Percy, as he watched the Roy and Loy futilely first bouncing a mattock and then a pick ax off of the solid rock wall at the back of the overhang.

After exhausting themselves and accomplishing almost nothing, the group decided that there must be a better way. Roy Potter sat down on one end of a mossy pine log, his brother Loy straddled the other end, and Percy positioned himself on a large flint rock a few feet away from the log. In the stillness of the damp pine forest the three began to meditate seriously. The quart of moonshine that Roy had thoughtfully brought along was sure to provide some inspiration.

Then Loy truly was inspired! "We bein' jus' plain stupid," he declared. "Over at the house, we got a bunch of dynamite that Daddy brought back from West Virginia. We'll jest blast us a big ole hole in the side of that there ridge and that'll be it. See you fellers in a little bit."

Loy stood up and shuffled away through the piney woods and towards Percy's house. A minute later, Percy and Roy could hear Loy's truck as it cranked up and rumbled out toward the main road.

Neither Percy nor Roy said a word for a while, both feeling embarrassed that they had not thought of the obvious solution. They just sat there silently in the woods, first one and then the other sipping the potent clear liquid from the canning jar. After about half an hour, they heard Loy's truck coming back down the drive, but by that time, unfortunately, neither Percy nor Roy was in any condition to perform any serious work on the project.

"Looka-here what I got," announced Loy, appearing through the pines while holding up four sticks of dynamite in his huge left hand. "I got caps and fuses too. And look here what else I got." Loy swung around to reveal Boomer the Cat, tucked under his right arm. "Is this here yore cat?" he asked. "Hit was a'sleepin' on the hood of yore car."

That sum-bitch," growled Percy, stumbling toward Loy and the cat. "He's ruining my car. I'm gonna fix that damn cat once and for all. Give me a stick of that dynamite."

Loy and Roy were at first reluctant to participate in what Percy obviously had in mind, but at his insistence, Loy held Boomer while Percy tied a stick of the dynamite to the cat's tail with a piece of twine. Percy then crimped a detonation cap onto about two feet of fuse with his teeth and pushed the cap into the end of the stick of dynamite.

"I don't think this is real good idea," Loy kept insisting,

but he continued to hold on to the squirming cat.

Percy was not by nature a cruel man, but his hatred for Boomer the Cat combined with his state of inebriation had totally perverted his judgment. "I've had it with this here cat. I'm gonna get shet of him for good this time," he announced, as he struck a match and lit the fuse. "Let him go Loy," he shouted.

At the exact same second that Loy released the cat, they all heard a car door slam. The sound of the door was followed by the voices of Mrs. Whittaker and the children as they returned from church. Boomer the Cat was now headed for the house as fast as he could go, terrified by the spewing fuse trailing out behind his long tail.

Percy stood paralyzed for only a second, as an awful reality swept over him. Then he lit out running through the woods and toward the house as fast as he could manage, while screaming at the top of his lungs. "Get away from the house! The cat's a'comin'! Get away! Get away! The cat's a'comin'! The cat's a'comin'!"

As she climbed the steps to the front porch, Mrs. Whittaker heard Percy's screams coming from behind the house, but she could simply not imagine why anyone should get so excited about the arrival of Boomer the Cat.

As the cat approached the house, Percy ran frantically after him, continuing to scream "the cat's a'comin', the cat's a'comin'!" A few yards short of the house, just as Boomer disappeared under the back porch, Percy tripped on a tree root and went sprawling. About a second later, just as Mrs. Whittaker opened the front door and started into the house, a terrific explosion erupted under the back porch, blowing the porch roof skyward and reducing the rest of the dilapidated porch structure to kindling wood. The house seemed to jump about a foot off its foundation and then rattle back down, leaving a heap of broken lumber where the porch had been, the back door hanging from one hinge, and most of the windows on the back side of the house shattered. Mrs. Whittaker was knocked backwards through the front door by the blast, and she ended up seated heavily on the front porch floor in a most undignified position.

As a suddenly sober and frightened Percy ran into the parlor and looked out through the front door, he was greeted by a view of Mrs. Whittaker, solidly seated on the front porch. She may have been stunned, but she was already glaring at Percy as though she knew that all of this was his doing and that there was going to be hell to pay. Fortunately, she appeared to be unhurt, and the children, who were all out in the front yard when the blast occurred were not injured.

Everyone was numbed by the shock of the explosion, with the wife and the children all wondering what on earth could have happened. The only thing Percy, obviously the perpetrator of the chaos, could think to say to his wife was "How was church today, Dear?"

As a contrite Percy sheepishly attempted to explain what had happened, the rest of the family became increasingly furious, with Mrs. Whittaker leading the attack. It was by the Grace of God that none of them had been killed by such a stupid, violent act, she declared. It was another item on her long, long list of examples of destruction created by the influence of alcohol. The damage to the house could be repaired, but the very idea of attaching dynamite to any animal, especially the family pet, was the most callous, dangerous, and inhumane thing anyone ever heard of.

As Mrs. Whittaker continued to berate Percy, Loy and Roy stood amid the debris in the living room, looking meekly at each other and nodding in agreement with every word she said. As Percy was humbly submitting to the scorching indictment being inflicted by his wife, the Whittaker children were all out in front of the house, wailing and sobbing over the loss of their beloved kitty.

Percy tearfully agreed with his all of his wife's pronouncements regarding his selfishness and depravity and pleaded for forgiveness. He proclaimed himself, from that very moment, to be a changed man, swearing perpetual abstinence from alcohol and promising to get the children a new kitty, among other things.

Percy helped Mrs. Whittaker up and onto her feet, but without even responding to her husband's pleas of contrition, Mrs. Whittaker turned her back to him and stumped off the front porch and down the steps into the yard. Percy stood humbly on the front porch contemplating the emotional and physical damage, that he had brought down on his home and family. Then, with his head drooping forward and his hat in his hand, he slowly and shamefully walked back inside to assess the damage to the house.

A loud cheer that erupted from in front of the house suddenly snapped Percy back into wakefulness. The cheer was followed by the sound of excited chatter and shouts of laughter. With the frightening thought that someone might have suffered a head injury and was delusional, Percy ran back out of the house and into the front yard. There he found his children joyfully jumping around, laughing and clapping their hands.

"Would you look at that, Percy. Can you believe it?"

cried Mrs. Whittaker, laughing and pointing toward his car. "Do you suppose he has eight more lives?"

There, calmly perched on the hood of Percy's shiny Ford Coupe, licking his paws as though nothing out of the ordinary had happened, sat a singed and dirty, but aloof and unrepentant, Boomer the Cat.

"Oh, I'm so glad he's all right. I'll take him to the veterinarian and have him checked to be sure. Oh, My Dear, can you ever forgive me?" At the moment, Percy was completely sincere in his remorse about the cat, although it was likely to have been only temporary.

"Well…maybe, just maybe, someday I will be able to forgive you." Mrs. Whittaker conceded. "But that will be someday **after** you have built me a new back porch."

Well, between Scotch and nothin', I suppose I'd take Scotch. It's the nearest thing to good moonshine I can find these days.

William Faulkner

Secret Formula

The Mayberry Store did a booming business during the few years that the City of Danville Hydroelectric Project and the Blue Ridge Parkway were both under construction in Mayberry, but around 1940, after the projects were all completed, business really slowed down. Then, just a couple of years later, the country became engaged in the Second World War, and that conflict caused all kinds of changes everywhere, even including Mayberry.

A number of the young men from the community went into military service, while some other folks, both men and women, began working away in war related jobs at defense plants in places like Martinsville and Norfolk, Virginia, and Oak Ridge, Tennessee. Some of the money from these jobs that was paid to folks from Mayberry did find its way back home, so there was no real shortage of cash at that time. But a lot of other problems were created when everyday goods such as sugar and gasoline, commodities that had always been a big part of the store's business, began being rationed by the government. The limits that rationing placed on so many basic goods really cut into what folks were able to buy at the store, even when they had the money.

The difficulty encountered by the owner of the Mayberry Store in trying to conduct anything near its normal trade and supplying the needs of its customers was just one example of how the war effort was affecting almost every business in the country. By 1943, if someone in Mayberry needed a new tube of toothpaste, they had to bring the old empty tube to the store with them. The squeeze tubes for toothpaste were made of tin back then, and the old tube either had to be traded for a customer to get a new tube of toothpaste, or the customer would have to go home with a can of tooth powder. Not only were sugar and gasoline being rationed, but coffee, tobacco, butter, and shoes were soon added to the limited availability list.

Lloyd and John were an interesting pair of customers, with Lloyd as tall and thin as a fence rail, and John a foot shorter and toting a belly that hung out over his belt buckle. The two came into the store together so often that the store regulars began referring to them as "Mutt and Jeff," a name taken from the two characters featured in the popular cartoon strip by that name and who were likewise defined by their contrasting physiques.

When the two strode into the Mayberry Store on that early spring morning in 1944, they were obviously on a quest. "Hey Mr. Coy, how much sugar can you let us have today?" Lloyd asked, pulling out his brand new book of U.S. Government ration stamps. Just a few days before, Lloyd and John had bought up all of the quart-sized Mason jars the store had in stock, so it was obvious to Mr. Yeatts and all of the hangers-on around the store just what Lloyd and John were up to. John had also bought the only copper canning boiler the store had in stock a few months before, and it was a good thing that he bought it when he did, because the store didn't have another copper boiler until sometime in 1946.

"Well, that depends," Coy Yeatts, proprietor of the

Mayberry Store, seriously informed the two. “I think we could let you have two pounds for yourselves and two more pounds for each of your wives if both of you are married.” The proprietor then chuckled, “but you can only buy two pounds each if you are married to each other.”

Coy Yeatts’ calculation created a snort of laughter among the loafers sitting around the warm wood stove in the middle of the store. The joke was especially funny to them because, for the last couple of years, anytime anyone had seen either John or Lloyd, it had almost always been in the company of the other. But everyone in the store also knew that the two were always seen together because they were business partners. Lately, however, they seemed to have had some serious problems getting the raw materials they needed to keep their business going.

Although John had planted a few acres of corn the previous spring, it had been a dry year and there had not been much of a crop. Lloyd had never even tried to grow any corn. The partners had run out of the most basic raw material required for making moonshine several months before. But now, the combination of factors, including the bad season for corn and government rationing that made legal whisky all but impossible to obtain, both the demand and the price for the locally made hooch had taken a big jump. This was a really good time to be in the business of making corn likker, if only you could get hold the stuff you needed to make it. With warm weather approaching, Lloyd and John were desperate to get their still fired up and running again.

“How about Lloyd’s young’un?” John, who normally did most of the dealing, asked Coy. “Can we get a sugar ration for him?”

"You can if you have the stamps," a serious Coy Yeatts told them, as he carefully unfolded the sheet of paper he had recently been sent by the U.S. Government. The sheet detailed the most recent information concerning the current rules about what was now being rationed and how much of each commodity could legally be sold to each individual or household. Sugar had been one of the first things to be rationed when the program was begun in 1942, and the current allotment was one pound of sugar per person per week. Lloyd's ration book contained fifty six number 30 ration stamps, but no more than two could be used within a single week. On the other hand, each farm family was allotted twenty-five pounds of sugar per year for canning, but there was just one special stamp in each book for that. According to the most recent rationing regulations, regulations to which a very patriotic Coy Yeatts carefully adhered, Lloyd and John could theoretically purchase 60 pounds of sugar together that day, but that would be all they could buy for several weeks

Again John pulled his book of ration stamps from his back pocket. "Jetty says we need sugar too," he announced, but his book contained only a few of the precious number 30 ration stamps. Coy figured that theoretically, John and Lloyd could legally purchase sixty-six pounds of sugar, enough to start up three to five barrels of mash, depending on what they could find to ferment along with it. He was less than sympathetic with the problems these guys were having, even though the supplies such as the Mason jars and sugar that Lloyd and John often bought from the Mayberry Store made a significant contribution to his business. Coy did not think too highly of folks that dealt with moonshine, either as producers or consumers. He held a special contempt for moonshiners such as Lloyd and John, men who had the potential to make lot more money from the sale of their illegal whisky, if they would just not drink such a large part of what they made. Their personal consumption cut deeply into the profit they were able to take home. But as folks used to say, "Never buy likker from a moonshiner that don't drink his own stuff.

Anyway, Coy had a large family of his own to support, and if he didn't sell John and Lloyd the raw materials for their business, he knew that there were other stores that would sell them everything they needed.

It also irritated Coy that the two moonshiners wanted to use up all of their ration stamps at one time. Not only did it leave the moonshiners unable to buy any more sugar for a while, but it left the Mayberry Store in short supply for its other customers. Looking over the counter at the two ration books that had been presented to him and then looking at the dwindling supply of sugar on the store shelves behind him, Coy made a quick calculation. "Let's see Lloyd, I know you've got a wife and a young'un. And John, you live in a household with your sister Jettie, so it looks like together you have enough of the red stamps to buy sixty-six pounds of sugar. But Sugar is getting harder and harder to come by, you know, and just so I won't be running out in a week or two, I think I can only let the two you have fifty pounds of sugar. You can buy that much now by just using your canning stamps, and then you can buy more later on."

Lloyd was very unhappy with Mr. Coy's decision. "Well then, maybe we'll just take our business out to the Meadows of Dan Store," he threatened.

"Well now, you can do what you have to do," Coy retorted. "But I don't think they have a whole lot more sugar than we do. Tom Agee might not even sell you that much. And you will have to have the stamps for whatever you buy, wherever you buy it. So you can buy your sugar here, or you can buy it there, but you won't be able to buy a whole bunch of it at both places."

Although they were not too happy about it, Lloyd and John paid Mr. Coy sixty-five cents each for five ten-pound bags of sugar, and it was a given that they were planning to go on out to Meadows of Dan and see how much more they could buy at Agee's Store. As they carried the bags out to Lloyd's pickup, they handled them like precious cargo, carefully packing the sugar onto the seat between them. Lloyd drove his pickup away from the Mayberry Store with John carefully holding the bags of sugar onto the seat with both hands.

Early the very next morning, the two men were back at the store. "Hey, Mr. Coy!" John boomed as he walked into store. "Chicken Scratch and Milk Maker Sweet Cow Feed ain't being rationed yet are they?"

"No John, not the last time I checked anyways. I figger if it comes a time when the government starts rationing chicken feed, we are really in a mess of trouble," the proprietor responded.

"How much have you got?" John wanted to know. Apparently, John and Lloyd had been communicating with someone who had shared some recent developments in the finer points of modern moonshining.

"Well, I'll have to check," Coy Yeatts thought out loud, "we're running kind of low. I think we maybe have a dozen bags of the scratch feed and a half dozen bags of the laying mash. Those are both fifty pound bags. We don't have more than eight or ten of the hundred pound bags of Milk Maker cow feed though, and that's all the cow chop we have in stock."

"How much is it a bag, for a bag of each kind of feed?" John wanted to know.

"A hundred pound bag of cow chop is now a dollar ten," Coy responded. "It's gone way up since the war started. The scratch is still forty cents a bag and the laying mash is still sixty five, but I'm guessing that you don't need no mash."

John and Lloyd both appeared to be shocked at the prices they had just been quoted. "We gotta' think about that," John responded. The two men moved back outside and stood in front of the store, putting their heads together and engaging a serious discussion. Most everyone knew that chicken scratch could be used to make moonshine, but using cow feed was a new idea, at least it was in Mayberry.

It has often been said that desperate times produce desperate solutions, and Lloyd and John had learned from someone that certain kinds of the bagged feed for dairy cattle contained starchy material that would ferment pretty well. Not only that, but mixed into Milk Maker Sweet Cow Feed was a significant amount of brewers' yeast and a small quantity of black strap molasses. The fact that the feed was advertised to contain large amounts of protein, calcium, and vitamins that were guaranteed to stimulate milk production, however, was of no interest to Lloyd and John. The most important thing about any kind of feed was the grain it contained, but the brewers' yeast and molasses in the cow feed might also be a big plus for using it to make liquor.

"We got some figgerin' to do," Lloyd announced. Lloyd and John then engaged in another serious conference outside in front of the store, with Lloyd using a stub of a pencil to do some scribbling in the VC Fertilizer pocket notebook he always carried. After a few minutes of argument, the two confidently returned to the store counter.

"We'll take all of your chicken scratch and all of your sweet cow feed," announced John.

Even though it was not officially being rationed, Coy had to tell the guys that he couldn't let all of the chicken feed and cow feed in the store to go to a single customer. He only got a feed delivery every two weeks, and with the war going on, there was no telling what might be rationed next. Coy Yeatts figured it was more important for his other customers to have sufficient feed for their livestock than it was for a pair of sorry moonshiners to use up all of the available animal feed in the process of making what was almost certainly going to be some of the lowest grade hooch ever made in Mayberry.

"Well, I just can't sell you all of it right at once," Coy told them. "I've got other customers that will be needing feed before the truck from Mt. Airy gets back up here. But if you want to order some more in advance, I can probably get you all you can use in a week or two."

When the two men finally came back into the store and walked over to the counter, it was Lloyd's turn to be the negotiator. "Mr. Coy, how much is your hog feed?"

"Well, the Triple X Daisy Middlings is seventy-five cents for a hundred pound bag and the Double X is forty cents for a fifty pound bag. Most people buy the triple X, and we do have plenty of that." Now it appeared as though John and Lloyd were going to try and develop some of their own recipes for moonshine. Although it was known that some cow feed that contained ingredients that could be used to make drinkable moonshine, the usefulness of the wheat middlings-based hog feed as a raw material was somewhat more innovative.

Lloyd and John conferred again for a minute or two before John asked how much of the Daisy Middlings Hog Feed they could buy.

After a few more minutes of haggling, Coy agreed to sell them six bags of the sweet cow feed, ten bags of chicken scratch, and a dozen bags of the triple-X Daisy Middlings. “That comes to eighteen dollars and sixty cents, but if you are hauling it yourselves, I’ll knock off the sixty cents,” he told them.

With no further discussion, John peeled off eighteen dollars from a roll of one dollar bills and paid for an amount of animal feed that was about the equivalent what the Mayberry Store would have sold in a normal week. John had an account at the Mayberry Store that he usually paid off at the end of every month, but he had paid cash for the sugar the day before and was now paying cash for a ton of animal feed. Coy was sure that John and Lloyd were in a business venture financed by some third unknown individual.

As Coy Yeatts rolled out bags of feed on a hand truck, four at a time, Lloyd and John loaded them into the sagging bed of Lloyd’s ’36 Ford pickup. After they had loaded a dozen bags, Coy became concerned as he noticed how low the rear end of the pickup was sagging. Mr. Yeatts was a businessman, but he was also concerned about the welfare of his customers. “Lloyd, don’t you reckon that all of this feed might be too much weight on your truck?" he asked.

"Naw, this here's a tough ol' truck, "Lloyd insisted. I've hauled a bunch more than this. We'll throw ten more bags on'er if you'll let us have 'em."

"Can't let you have all the feed. There's other folks who'll be needing some too." Coy repeated. "But the truck from Mt. Airy should be here a week from Friday. Just tell me how many bags you want and I'll have 'em right here for you then."

"Coy Yeatts had figured out that the sugar he had just sold these characters would be barely enough to make a couple of runs of sugarhead likker, maybe enough to net about forty or fifty gallons. He didn't know a whole lot about making moonshine, but he knew that if a 'shiner had enough sugar to get a batch started, there was a lot of other stuff that could be fermented well enough to make likker that was good enough for folks who weren't too particular about what they drank. In addition to the sugar, corn was the preferred ingredient, but growing, shucking, shelling, and sprouting corn took a lot of work. He had overheard enough conversations in the store to know that sweet cow feed would ferment well enough to make a drinkable form of moonshine. He had overheard conversations that claimed that a hundred pound bag of the fourteen percent Milk Maker could make five to eight gallons of moonshine, if the fermentation was started with five or ten pounds of sugar. Now as far as using Daisy Middlings to make drinkable moonshine was concerned, he had his doubts.

Lloyd and John loaded down Lloyd's little half-ton truck with almost a ton of feed, six one-hundred pound cloth sacks of cow feed on the bottom, ten fifty-pound bags of chicken scratch on top of that, and it all topped off with a dozen sacks of Daisy Middlings hog feed. Lloyd and John headed out in great spirits, the little Ford pickup chugging and smoking up Mayberry Road.

Unfortunately, as Lloyd attempted to turn onto Rt. 600 at the Mayberry Church, he was going way too fast for the load the truck was carrying. The load of feed shifted over to one side in the pickup bed, causing the sagging bed to scrub right through the already-bare right rear tire. When the tire blew out, the little old truck careened across the road and turned over onto its side, dumping the sacks of feed into the middle of the intersection of Mayberry Road and Rt. 600. About half of the paper sacks of Daisy Middlings burst on impact, causing a huge cloud of the hyperfine hog feed to erupt into the surrounding air.

It was a good thing that the Atomic Bomb had not been invented yet, because if it had, the mushroom cloud produced by that truck wreck would have frightened the residents of Mayberry plumb to death. It may be that one has to have had some experience dealing with XXX Daisy Middlings to appreciate what an incredibly fine powder it is. Daisy Middlings was just about the finest powder that could be made by the grain milling machinery of that time, with the XXX indicating that the wheat middlings had been run through a roller mill three times, creating a powder that is ten times finer than talcum. Until the water has been added to Triple-X Middlings, the slightest puff of wind will produce a cloud of fine, light brown powder that will naturally adhere to almost any surface with which it comes in contact due to static electricity. The rupture of the bags of Daisy Middlings in the middle of the Mayberry road produced a mushroom cloud that looked like a miniature of the cloud that would be produced by the first atomic bomb about a year later. Then, a gusty wind hit the burst bags, scattering the fine powder in all directions and giving a coating to the road, the ground, the nearby vegetation, and even to the Mayberry Church. The middlings was all over everything that was anywhere near the accident.

Neither John nor Lloyd was hurt. They both climbed up and out of the pickup through the driver's side window, jumped down from the side of the truck, and eased out through the slough of the middlings to try and survey the damage. What they now had was about the biggest mess anyone had ever seen. John walked down the Mayberry road to the store, where he was able to recruit a couple of the loafers to come help him and Lloyd right the truck. He also borrowed a couple of shovels from Coy to try and salvage some of the spilled hog feed.

The truck appeared to have suffered little damage to its rusted and already well-dented fenders and doors. The sky was clouding up, so after the truck was righted, Lloyd and John began working like crazy to salvage as much of the Daisy Middlings as they could, shoveling it up off the road and back into the bed of the pickup. A few of the paper hog feed bags were not damaged, and a few more were punctured but still held most of their original contents, but it took Lloyd and John several hours to convert the pile of sacks and the spilled feed that was in the road into a pile of sacks and loose feed in the back of the pickup. In the process, both of the men had become coated with the fine powder from head to toe; they looked like a couple of well-tanned ghosts as they frantically worked to rescue their moonshine raw material.

The two had just decided they had rescued as much of the hog feed as was practical when the next worst thing that could happen, did happen. Before Lloyd could get the flat tire on his pickup changed, it began to rain. If you are not a farm person and have never mixed XXX Daisy Middlings with water for the purpose of feeding hogs, then you can't possibly appreciate the sloughy mess it created there in the road. It was only a brief shower, but afterward, the men, the road, and the pickup were covered with one of the most disgusting viscous fluids ever produced by American agricultural ingenuity. Daisy Middlings powder mixed with water combines the normally contradictory properties of being viscous, slimy, and sticky all at the same time. If you step in it, you will almost certainly slip down, but if you try to wipe it off, it is removable just one layer at a time, for layer after layer. For all the world, a mix of XXX Daisy Middlings and water has all of the same disgusting properties as slug mucous. If you have ever stepped on a Giant Carolina Slug with your bare feet, then possibly you can appreciate the fluid properties of Daisy Middlings.

The two would-be moonshiners were in middle of the biggest mess anyone in Mayberry had ever seen; they were coated from head to toe with the slimy fluid, and the contents of the pickup bed was largely converted into a load of the goo. A large patch of the Mayberry Road was coated with such a layer of the middlings glop that it presented a significant hazard for weeks. When the highway department sent a couple of men out to scatter some sand over the mess in the road, the sand just created a gritty slime in the road that was stranger than ever.

No one, other than the 'shiners themselves, ever knew

how much of the original load of animal feed Lloyd and John were able to actually use for the purpose of making moonshine, but it was almost certainly more than they should have used. The cow feed may have been entirely salvageable, but at least half of the Daisy Middlings was lost, and that was probably for the best. I have to imagine that just mixing up mash using the middlings hog feed must have been really difficult, given how the middlings sticks to everything it touches. It seems likely that just disposing of spent mash made from Daisy Middlings would be really difficult and disgusting job.

A couple of months after the accident with Lloyd's pickup, Allen Spence came into the Mayberry Store one morning, and he was obviously not feeling well. "Mr. Coy, you got anything for an awful bellyache?" he asked.

As Coy Yeatts handed him a bottle of soda mint tablets, Allen added, "And I need somethin' for one helluva headache too!

As Mr. Coy turned and reached toward the shelf that held the aspirin, he asked Allen about the nature of his complaints. Did he think he had the flu?

"Ahhh, it ain't that. It ain't the flu. I just should'a knowed better," Allen confided to Coy. "I'd been told that Lloyd and John had been runnin' off some really awful moonshine of late. I'd heard so much about how bad it was that I wasn't even goin' to buy none of it. But nobody else has anything at all to sell, so Friday I broke down and bought a half gallon from John. Oh! Man! I've been payin' for it ever since."

"Well, I think I can tell you what the problem is," Coy confided. "Lloyd and John, why they've been makin' their stuff out of cow chop and chicken feed and everything else you can think of. Why, they're even makin' moonshine usin' Daisy Middlings hog feed!"

Allen looked a little puzzled and then he asked, "What's that you say? What's about Daisy Middlings? What is that?"

Coy explained to Allen, "Daisy Middlings is a kind of hog feed. Lloyd and John have been making some of their moonshine using hog slop!"

Allen sadly shook his head, but then he managed a wry smile. "Well, I'm sure glad you told me that," he admitted. "I figgered that anything` as bad as that stuff John sold me must have been made usin' hog shit."

Oklahomans will continue to vote dry for as long as they can stagger to the polls.

Will Rogers

What's Cooking?

Fred had survived the war physically intact, but the time he had spent with the United States Army fighting all the way across Europe had left him with a basic outlook on things and a low tolerance for nonsense. When he finally came home to Virginia, though, he was lucky enough to find the girl he left behind, waiting there just for him. About a year later, after Fred had been able to leave his demons behind, he and Georgia got married. He even found a job driving a truck for Agee's General Store and Farm Supply, pretty good employment for the time and place.

Five years later and now the father of two young kids, Fred began building the family a house in Mayberry. Fred was doing a lot of the work himself, so progress on the couple's dream home was kind of slow, but a couple of years after the project was begun, the family was able to move in. For Fred and Georgia, their little house in Mayberry was a dream come true.

The house might have been modest by modern city standards, but it had a few niceties that folks in Mayberry could only have dreamed about before the war. The lap siding covered bungalow had a front porch view that faced out toward the Mayberry Road, and from the back stoop you could hear the rippling music of Round Meadow Creek. There was no electric power available in Mayberry until 1949, but now the year was 1951, and every room of their modern home was equipped with an electric ceiling light and two or three electrical outlets. The house had electrically heated water, an indoor bathroom, and a kitchen equipped with the latest electric appliances. Not only did the kitchen have a refrigerator, but it had something that Georgia had been thinking about since she was a young girl. As a teenager, Georgia had stayed with her aunt in Richmond for a time, and the aunt had a 1930's version of the modern all-electric kitchen.

The thing about the aunt's kitchen that had impressed Georgia the most was the electric range, a cooking stove not all that different from the one that was now installed in the kitchen of her Mayberry dream home. The new electric range – it was a range, not a stove, the home demonstration agent had sternly informed her – had three burners and a deep fryer on top, a large oven, a small oven, and all kinds of modern electric gizmos. Georgia could never have figured out how to operate the clock, the timer, the alarm, and all that technology without the assistance provided by the home demonstration agent sent from Appalachian Electric Power Company.

When Georgia told Fred about how helpful the lady from the power company had been, Fred replied that he figured the agent from the power company had been trained to teach homemakers how to use as much electric power as possible.

Sometimes, when things seem too good to be true, they really are. The owner of the business where Fred worked died suddenly, and the store had to be closed down until everything could be reorganized. Fred's job of driving a truck for the store stopped, of course, and he could not find another good job nearby. With a growing family, VA loan payments to make, and indebtedness looming, Fred fell back on a course of action that had been the solution for several people he had known. If a man had the right contact – perhaps a family member who belonged the United Mine Workers – there was a fair chance that he could find some kind of a job in the coal fields of West Virginia.

Fred headed for Beckley, West Virginia, leaving his wife and children on their own in Mayberry for a time. When he left, Fred did promise Georgia that he would look for a job "above ground," rather than applying for the more dangerous underground work in the mines. He had no idea how his job search might turn out, but in his previous job and while in service, he had gained a lot of experience in driving different types trucks. Because of this background, Fred had little trouble in landing a job driving a coal truck. They thought of Beckley as kind of a rough place, so the original plan had been for Fred to leave Georgia and the girls behind in Mayberry and come home on the weekends. Unfortunately, Fred's new job required that he work at least every other weekend, and he was soon missing his wife and family something terrible. But Fred's luck held and he was able to find an acceptable little house for rent near Beckley. Without even talking with Georgia about it first, he signed a lease on the house and then spent his next free weekend moving his family to West Virginia.

The assumption from the beginning was that the West Virginia job was just a temporary situation and that as soon as things got straightened out, they would all be back, living in their home in Mayberry. The house that Fred had rented near Beckley was basically furnished, so the family had to bring a just few things with them when they moved to West

Virginia. At first, they were concerned about leaving their house unattended in Mayberry, but Fred's Uncle Percy lived nearby, and he had assured them that he would keep a close watch on their Mayberry house. Uncle Percy said he would check on the house every single day, if Fred and Georgia wanted him to.

The little family from Mayberry was soon settled into a very different life in Beckley, West Virginia, and they were reasonably comfortable there. The family had few real worries and life went well for the next few months. Fred was making good money in Beckley, and he was never a man to hang out at the beer joints and get into trouble. He was able to pay the rent in Beckley, keep up the payments on the house in Mayberry, and even put a little bit of money away. But he and Georgia sure did miss their home in Mayberry.

Then one month, when they got the mail that had been forwarded to them, they had an electric power bill for the Mayberry house that was for over sixty dollars! When they had been living in that house, the electric bill had never been more than fifteen dollars a month, and most months it had been about ten! Before leaving, they had cut off the water heater and unplugged the refrigerator, so the only thing that would be using any electric power was the low-wattage light bulb they had left on just to make it look like the house was occupied. (That was just in case there were some strangers passing through anyway, since everyone in Mayberry knew that the Fred and Georgia were now living in West Virginia.) Fred decided he had better make a trip back to Mayberry and find out what was wrong.

The next Saturday morning, Fred drove into Meadows of Dan and turned down the Mayberry Road for the last few miles to home. When he turned from the road and into the driveway and pulled up to the side their little mountain home, everything looked just fine at first. But he did think it was strange when he saw that his Uncle Percy's pickup was pulled all the way into the driveway and parked up real close behind the house.

As soon as Fred got out of his car, he was hit by a strong smell that was coming from three large wooden barrels that were sitting right up against the back of his house. Fred didn't have any use for big barrels like those, so what were they doing there? As Fred approached the back door, he could hear country music playing on a radio and see that there was a bright light burning in the kitchen, He knew that they had not left a radio playing or that light burning when they left. Was someone having a party in his house? Had someone moved into the house and was living there while he and his family were away? Or was Uncle Percy just really making himself at home?

When Fred started to unlock the kitchen door, he was surprised to find it already unlocked. Concerned, but not really afraid, Fred shoved the kitchen door open and rushed inside. There, standing right in front of Georgia's almost new electric range and looking very surprised was Fred's Uncle Percy.

Fred was surprised too, especially when he saw the contraption that was sitting on top of the electric range. Georgia's copper canning boiler was placed across the front of the range, with each end positioned on a burner. There was a smaller vessel sitting on the top of the range right behind the boiler and connected to it by a short length of copper pipe that had been soldered into the boiler lid. There was also a trail of smaller copper tubing running from the second vessel across the corner of the kitchen and connected to a whole bunch of copper tubing coiled inside of a keg that was setting in the sink. A short piece of water hose ran from the faucet and into the keg.

A large wooden barrel, full of something that smelled like beer and setting on the floor right in front of the kitchen range, told the tale. Uncle Percy was running a moonshine still in the kitchen of Fred and Georgia's otherwise unoccupied Mayberry dream house!

At the very moment Fred had walked in, Uncle Percy had been standing in front of the range, caught red handed as he used a stew pot to ladle the fermented wash from the barrel on the floor into the copper boiler on the range. It goes without saying that Georgia's usually spotless linoleum kitchen floor and her white enameled electric range were quite a mess! For a moment, neither Fred nor Uncle Percy quite knew what to make of the situation. They stood there gawking at each other, with Fred getting more upset by the second. Finally, he let loose; "Uncle Percy, just what in the hell do you think you're doin' here? Is this the way you've been lookin' after my house?"

"Well, well, well now," stammered Uncle Percy, "I've sure got it lookin' like there's somebody a-stayin' here ain't I? There ain't nobody goin' to be messin' around your place while I'm in here a'runnin off a little batch!"

Preacher Floyd

"Preacher! Hey Preacher! We need your help! Miz Bowman thinks she's a-dyin' and she sent us to get you. Can you come help her Preacher? Miz Bowman wants to make sure she's saved before she passes on. Can you please come talk to her, Preacher?"

When the preacher heard the plea for assistance coming from outside his front door, he did not hesitate. He had already been in his bed for hours and was sleeping soundly when he heard the cry for help, but he jumped from the bed and began hastily putting on his clothes.

"Just give me a minute. I'll be right there," he shouted back to the voice outside. If he had the time to count them up, the preacher knew three or four community women who could have been the "Miz Bowman" said to be in distress, and he had no idea which of them this one might be. But whomever she might be was not the point; his services were needed and he would serve the call. "Hold on, hold on. I'll be there in a minute." The Reverend Samuel P. Floyd reached deep into the closet to retrieve his clean clerical shirt and he then pulled his Sunday best clerical collar from the top dresser drawer. Almost anytime he left his home, the preacher was dressed in his clerical garb, but this occasion called for his very best.

For all the years he had been living there in the

community, Preacher Floyd had been called upon to offer spiritual sustenance only a few times, and this was his very first call from someone who was about to breath their last. His services were so rarely sought that he sometimes felt disrespected by the community, but here was a call that was not to be denied. He was thinking about how he could best provide consolation and peace of mind for the unfortunate woman as he slipped the stiffly starched collar around his neck and struggled to press the stud into place. Once successful with that, he turned the collar around and adjusted it carefully. He gave the collar a final tug, slipped on his best Sunday clerical jacket, and headed out the door.

There was no pole lamp near anyone's home in the mountains in 1950, so when The Reverend stepped outside of his front door, he could not see a thing beyond the shaft of light that was coming through the door opening. "Yes, yes, are you still there?" he called out to the darkness and closing the door behind him. Now, just the light from the window beside the door provided a small area of illumination within the totally black surroundings.

"Over here, Preacher," a voice called from the darkness. "We're over here by the truck. Come get in and we'll take you on over to Miz Bowman's place."

Although he could not see the truck, the preacher stepped confidently out into total darkness, fearlessly striding toward the road and the sound of the invisible voice, giving no consideration to the possibility that anything nefarious might be at hand. But two steps after he had entered the darkness, a disembodied voice shouted "now!" and the poor preacher was propelled backwards by a massive deluge of cold water.

Judging from the amount of water and the strength of the impact, he must have been hit by a full wash-tub of cold water, a tub full propelled with such force that it had to have been thrown by two strong men. The effect of this assault on the unsuspecting preacher was enough to send him into a state of emotional shock. The shock he felt was not just from the impact of the cold water, although that was trauma enough. But the more powerful shock was the humiliation and disrespect with which the poor preacher felt he was targeted. It was utter contempt, showered upon him as he left the comfort of his home and bed, embarking on what he had believed to be an opportunity to serve a fellow being. He had thought he was answering a call to render spiritual sustenance to a soul in need, and it was nothing more than a cruel prank. It was just one more affront to the dignity of a man who only wanted to be taken seriously and be recognized for the role he wished to fulfill, that of an humble servant of the Lord.

As Preacher Floyd fled from the deluge toward the refuge of his front door, he was hounded by humiliating guffaws from the perpetrators. He turned as he was retreating through his door and shook his fist at the darkness. “Heathen! Barbarians! Spawn of Satan!” He shouted, invoking the most profound indictments he was capable of projecting. The response from the darkness was only more laughter, followed by the slamming of the doors of a vehicle. Finally, as if even the sanctuary of his home was under siege, the preacher’s door was pelleted with a shower of gravel as the vehicle spun its wheels and sped off through the darkness.

It was a chilly evening, and the Preacher shivered as he

slammed the door shut and began pulling off his wet clothes. "Forgiveness is divine," he said to himself. "But with vandals like these running loose in the countryside, no one is safe. Something has to be done!" As soon as he had dried himself off and gotten back into his nightshirt, the preacher went into the kitchen and began vigorously cranking the handle of the wooden telephone box that hung on the wall. He had to crank out the two long rings for central about a dozen times before anyone at the switchboard answered. "Meadows of Dan Central," a sleepy voice finally responded.

"Ring up the Sheriff's Office," Reverend Floyd shouted into the mouthpiece of the telephone. "I wish to report a heinous assault!"

To some folks, a tub of water being thrown on the Good Reverend may have seemed to have mostly been a harmless prank, but that was certainly not how it felt to him. He feared that the water might just be the opening of a deluge of harassment directed at him and his faith. On the other hand, the dousing may have simply been the culmination of a minor feud between the preacher and some of his young neighbors.

When the preacher had first showed up in the community, no one seemed to be quite sure where he had come from, but some folks thought he had moved there from West Virginia. As it turned out, his wife was the daughter of a former resident, which explained how his family ended up occupying an old house on a small tract of hilly farmland. There was also a story told about how he was a former coal miner who, upon finding that he had the symptoms of the miners' dreaded black lung disease, had put his life in the hands of the Lord. Later, when a thorough physical exam failed to find any trace of the illness, he had decided that he had been granted a reprieve by the Lord and that he was being called to go forth and preach the Gospel.

There were several families in the community who had previously spent some years in West Virginia, when the men had been working in the coal mines. A few thought maybe they had seen or heard of him preaching somewhere around Welch. There was some gossip that the preacher had run into a problem with the way the collection money was being used at a church he was pastoring, but then, there were others who said that they didn't think Preacher Floyd had ever pastored a *real* church. Although some of the stories seemed plausible, I learned long ago that there are some folks who are real good at taking a little bit of information and weaving it into a more interesting and detailed saga.

Later, there was a lot of gossip in the community about the dustup the Reverend and his wife had when she took a job working at the Elastic Plant in Stuart. Even though the reverend didn't have a job and the family was struggling, he declared that the man of the house should be the breadwinner and that the woman's place was in the home. Even back then, a lot of folks sided with Mrs. Floyd, thinking that if the preacher wasn't going to get a job, the least he could do was look after the kids while his wife worked. But maybe things would get better for them when the preacher built the church for which he was always trying to collect money.

The preacher wasn't much of a fellow to work out of doors, and he even appeared to be a little on the puny side, although he had demonstrated that he could walk for miles when the need arose. It was clear right off that he didn't know anything much about farming, although he did give it a little bit of a try. Folks were pretty accommodating at first; neighbors helped out by plowing a garden patch for him and giving him vegetables and stuff, and some may have even donated a little money toward the church he said that he was going to build. He never planted much in the garden that was plowed for him though, and he didn't seem to be much interested in getting a real job.

The preacher always signed his name as "Rev. Samuel P. Floyd." Although no one ever seemed to know what the "P" stood for, it was an obvious joke that maybe his middle name was "Preacher." He told everyone he met that he would appreciate it if they would address him as "The Reverend Floyd," and while a few complied, he was mostly known as "Preacher Floyd" by those who held him in less regard. The gentleman was generally treated with the degree of respect the good citizens thought due to a man of the cloth, even though the denomination into which he had been ordained or how he had obtained his reverend credentials remained something of a mystery.

The Reverend had explained to those who had pointedly inquired about his denomination that he was a member of a small sect of objectors who had separated from the Church of the Brethren way back when it had reunited with the United Methodist Church. They had been among the few to adhere to what they considered to be the One True Original Faith, according to The Reverend, so the adherents thought it appropriate that they call their small denomination *The Remnant*. "The Remnant" could have meant a lot of things, but some folks figured it really meant that he and his family were of the few remaining members of whatever denomination it was that he had once belonged to. But "wearing a funny-lookin' collar don't automatically make somebody a Man of God," was a comment sometimes heard around Mayberry.

If you research the groups who call themselves "The Remnant" today, you will find that there are a number of religious and quasi-religious organizations that go by that name, but none of them would seem to fit in with the doctrine proscribed by The Reverend Floyd. If we'd had the internet back then, maybe we could have found out a little more about his denomination, but we had to make do with the school library, and the 1948 World Book Encyclopedia did not contain a word about any organization called "The Remnant". Some things we did learn about the denomination from Preacher Floyd's proselytizations were that the adherents to The Remnant doctrines did not smoke, drink, eat pork, or allow themselves to be photographed.

When the Good Reverend was asked about the no photograph business, he would connect it to a couple of scriptural quotes about "not making graven images." Preachers I had previously heard speak on the subject indicated that those verses referred to idolatry, but nobody was much bothered by the fact that he did not want either himself or his family to be photographed. That was a belief that was easy enough to respect, although there were a few murmurings that maybe the Reverend was worried that someone might compare a photograph of him to one posted on the wall in the Post Office.

The Preacher let it be known right away that he was looking for a place to start a new church, but of course, he had no funds. At first, he wanted to use the old Mayberry School building, but the county would not agree to that, since it had been closed in the first place because it was found to be unsafe. The Preacher also tried having services in an old barn that was on his place, but it was so drafty and rickety and so far off the road that nobody would attend. Then, he found out that the old store building located just about a mile down the road from his house was available. The rent was a kind of steep for a small dilapidated building that hadn't been used for years, but Preacher Floyd declared that it must be the place anyway.

When the reverend asked around for volunteers to help fix up the building, once again he found his neighbors to be very accommodating. The tin roof was still sound, which was good, and when some of the men cut the weeds around the building and put white lap siding over the tar paper on the front of the building, it improved the appearance of the place a lot. After a good neighbor built a small cupola onto the roof ridge right over the front door, it even began to look kind of like a little church. Other neighbors built wooden benches or contributed cane bottom chairs to seat the congregation. A neighbor who did carpentry even built an elevated podium and installed it at the end of the church opposite the door, creating the perfect place for the preacher to stand as he preached. A lot of folks thought it was a great thing, seeing a building that once held a store that sold beer and had a pool table, now converted into a house of worship.

The reverend himself nailed a piece of plywood onto the front of the building, painted it white, and got somebody to paint a message on it. In large red letters that ran all of the way across the top of the sign, the building was declared to be “THE CELESTIAL TABERNACLE.” Below, in smaller black letters, the sign revealed that, *Where sin did abound, now the Spirit doth abide.*

As the humble little structure began to take on a more church-like appearance, the preacher began to refer to it as *The Tabernacle,* and said it should remind folks of the humble circumstances into which Jesus Christ was born. Then Preacher Floyd declared that this was but the beginning, the beginning of the CELESTIAL CITY, the manifestation of heaven on earth, the place where the Lord would reign for the thousand years before the end of all time. That was when some of the folks in the community decided that the good reverend really had gone a little nutty. He said that he got the “Celestial City” business from somewhere in Revelations, and if folks seemed a little skeptical, it may have been because, while the building looked like it might have been good for another five or six years, it definitely would not last a thousand.

At the first Sunday’s service, the Celestial Tabernacle appeared to be off to an auspicious start. There must have been thirty or forty people there for the inaugural service, and that was not bad, considering that the total population of the community was only a couple of hundred souls. The euphoria that Reverend Floyd had felt when he saw his little church filled with people was not to last, however. There were several issues with the ministry, not the least of which was the fact that Preacher Floyd was something of a less than dynamic speaker. He was very nervous at the very first service in his new church, of course, and on this Sunday, he was more of a whisperer of the Gospel than a preacher. He obviously did not have a well-prepared message ready for the occasion. Indeed, even after all the neighbors had done for the Tabernacle, the Good Reverend spent the better part of the service appealing to the generosity of the little congregation and again begging for money. He talked on and on about what a long and difficult road he had travelled in his quest to found the Celestial City, but now that the Lord had chosen this particular place, he was sure that building the city was a goal that was within their reach. It simply required that the good people of the congregation open their hearts and their pocketbooks.

The people of the community had already shown how generous they were in the way they had helped him fix up the church building, but most of the folks to whom he was preaching really did not have a lot of worldly goods to share. The community had experienced a swift decline in population since the war, and the mostly elderly folk who still lived there needed to be careful with what little money they had. After the plate had been passed on that first Sunday, the benediction pronounced, and the congregation had dispersed, the Reverend found that the offering amounted to just a little more than ten dollars. And if the preacher found the contributions on that first Sunday to be less than encouraging, things only got worse. After about a month of services, a typical Sunday's take had dwindled down to about of five or six dollars, and for the next few months, the offering and everything else associated with the tabernacle just kept dwindling down. Most of the folks who had attended the church at its beginning were also affiliated with other, better established churches in the community, and they showed their confidence in the Reverend Floyd as a spiritual leader with their feet.

After a few months of the Reverend Floyd not paying the rent, the owner would not let him use the building anymore, and the Sunday services at the tabernacle came to an end. The sad little store turned into a church was closed up and there it sat, disused for month after month and rapidly returning to its former state of decay.

The Reverend would occasionally walk by the building, but seeing the forlorn little building that had once represented his fondest hopes just made him feel more lonely and depressed. One Saturday afternoon, however, as he walked past his former tabernacle, Preacher Floyd was surprised to see a couple of cars and a pickup parked beside it, and there was evidence of some activity on the inside. As the preacher approached the building, he slunk around the corner and stayed close to the wall, cautiously easing up to a window. The shades on the front windows were pulled all the way down, but he was able to peek in past the edge of one window shade. He could see several young men inside, all congregated in the center of the room, right beneath the single light bulb suspended from the ceiling. The men were sitting in chairs arranged on either side of a bench, and just a few moments of observation led the Reverend to the conclusion the bench was being used as a card table.

The Reverend could not only see that the young men were playing cards, but he could see that there was money lying on the bench onto which cards were being dealt, and he could see an open fruit jar sitting nearby. From time to time, one of the card players would lift the jar and take a swallow, sometimes offering it to another player seated near him. From the boisterous laughter and banter coming from within the tabernacle, the preacher figured that the jar must contain moonshine and he assumed that the young men must have been sipping from it for some time.

The poor preacher was aghast! The cycle was now complete! The little store building that had gone from being a den of iniquity into being a house of worship had now reverted back to being a place where gambling and drinking and riotous living were flourishing. His hope, his dream, his Celestial Tabernacle, was now being defiled in a most disgraceful manner. This would not do! The preacher shuffled back to his house as fast as he could manage, and as soon as he got inside, began cranking the telephone that hung on his kitchen wall. He vigorously cranked out the two long rings for central until someone at finally answered. He told the operator that he needed to be connected to the Sheriff's Office as quickly as possible. This was an emergency!

My sister and a girl cousin and I were out near the highway picking beans from our garden on a Saturday afternoon when two Sheriff's Department patrol cars came speeding past. Naturally, we wondered about what might have happened to require two patrol cars, but less than an hour later, the patrol cars came driving back by, each car now carrying several passengers in addition to the deputies who were driving.

My cousin and my sister were pretty teenaged girls at the time, and since it was a hot day, both of them were wearing short shorts. Political correctness had not yet been heard of in our community, so the occupants of the patrol cars responded just like any other bunch of uncouth teen-aged boys of the day. As the patrol cars drove past, the occupants leaned out of the open car windows and waved and whistled enthusiastically. Even the deputies got into the spirit of things, each driver giving a couple of quick bumps of his siren as he drove past.

The guys hanging out of the patrol car windows acted as though they were out on a lark, and my sister recognized several of them. "What kind of trouble have those boys gotten into this time?" she wondered out loud.

As soon as we got to school on Monday, we learned all about the trouble those boys were in. Everyone in school was talking about the Sheriff's department raiding the celestial tabernacle the previous Saturday. As it turned out, the guys who were inside the building were just a group of local teenage boys without much to do on a Saturday afternoon, and somebody had suggested that maybe they should organize a poker game. Not only had the boys obtained the owner's permission to use the Tabernacle building, he had even told them where to find the key. When the deputies came through the door of the tabernacle, there had been money lying on the bench, although the pitiful amount indicated that the boys must have been playing penny and nickel poker – just what the boys had claimed. There was an open but almost empty jar on the bench that may have contained a small amount of white liquor, but none of the boys appeared to be intoxicated. Unfortunately, both organized gambling and possession of untaxed spirits, especially by minors, were violations of both county and state statutes.

A few weeks later, when the boys appeared in court before the Trial Justice, the Honorable Ruth Williams, all of the boys admitted to gambling. Roscoe and Wesley, who were both eighteen, admitted to having consumed a small amount of liquor, which they claimed that they had found when they first entered the building. They also testified that none of the minors in the group had consumed any alcohol, which was not very likely. Judge Ruth threw out the illegal liquor charge on the basis of insufficient evidence, since nothing but fumes remained in the jar.

Following the Commonwealth Attorney's advice, all of the boys pleaded guilty to organized gambling and they were each assessed a $10.00 fine plus a court cost of $6.00 each. The fine was suspended on condition that the boys not commit any violations for a period of six months. In that time and place, the six dollar court cost was plenty of punishment for those kids, which was probably just what Judge Williams was thinking.

Everyone in the community soon found out about the boys getting busted for playing poker, but most folks just thought it was kind of funny and soon forgot about it. And a few months later, when the preacher got doused with cold water one night, no one knew anything about that incident until the story came out in a local newspaper.

According to the story printed in the *Patrick County Observer*, Preacher Floyd had told the Sheriff's Office that he was certain that his being assaulted with the cold water was directly related to his reporting of the gambling incident at his former Celestial Tabernacle. Since the assault occurred in total darkness, however, the preacher was unable to identify any of his cold water assailants. The morning after receiving the report from Preacher Floyd, the Sheriff had sent a deputy up to Reverend Floyd's residence to investigate, but the deputy could find little evidence to report. About the only significant things observed by the investigating officer were footprints outside the Preacher's house that appeared to have been made by someone who was wearing size 16 overshoes, and a set of tire tracks that led the officer to think that the perpetrators made their getaway in a pickup truck equipped with snow tread tires. The boys that had been arrested in the gambling raid were the most obvious suspects, but there was no physical evidence that connected them to the cold water assault on Reverend Floyd.

As soon as the story came out in the paper, everyone in the community who read about the size 16 galoshes figured that Roscoe Potter must have been involved. He was one of the older guys that had been arrested in the gambling raid, and he was also known to have the biggest feet of anyone around. The article reported the event as it was recorded by the Sheriff's Office, based on information provided by Reverend Floyd and the investigating deputies. The article in the paper reported that there was a $50.00 reward being offered for information leading to the apprehension and conviction of the culprits who threw the water on Reverend Floyd, but the last that I heard, no one had come forward with any helpful information.

Jimmy Price, the editor of weekly paper, was noted for his great sense of humor. The details of the cold water caper, including the fifty dollar reward, were all revealed in a story that covered most of front page of *The Patrick County Observer*, all printed under the banner headline announcing "THE REVEREND FLOYD GETS BAPTIZED!"

Prohibition may be the greatest gift any government ever gave its citizens. A barrel of beer cost $4 to make and sold for $55. A case of spirituous liquor cost $20 to produce and earned $90 – and all of this without taxes. Bill Bryson

Simple as ABC

The most recent job description for Virginia Bureau of Alcoholic Beverage Control Law Enforcement Agents indicates that the job includes not only responsibility for the enforcement of laws pertaining to the manufacture and distribution of alcoholic beverages, but it also includes responsibilities for the investigation of drug violations, gambling activity, gang activity, and even the enforcement of laws prohibiting the sale of cigarettes to minors.

Sixty years ago, there were no restrictions on the sale of cigarettes based on age, and the job description of the Virginia Alcoholic Beverage Control Law Enforcement Agent was entirely focused on the manufacture and distribution of alcoholic beverages. In the simplest of terms, the job of a Virginia State ABC Agent was to put bootleggers and moonshiners out of business. The function of their job was not one of improving the morality of the people of the county to which they were assigned, but simply to minimize the loss of the tax dollars that were supposed to be paid on all of the alcohol sold in that county. In those days, a name most feared by the moonshiners and bootleggers in Patrick County, Virginia, and the surrounding area was A.B. Clements, the State Alcoholic Beverage Control (ABC) Law Enforcement Agent assigned to that county.

While I know little about bootlegging and moonshining from firsthand experience, I did learn a few things about it secondhand, and much of what I learned was from tales I heard from my dad and his friends. Dad was never involved in any moonshine production or law enforcement either, but he was a mechanic who worked in the Salem District for the Virginia State Highway Department. The responsibilities of my dad's job included the maintenance and repair of state owned vehicles within the county. Among the many state owned vehicles he helped maintain were both the easily identifiable patrol cars used by the State Highway Patrol Officers and the official – but unmarked – cars used by other State Law Enforcement Officers assigned to the county. These included Virginia Game and Wildlife Officials and the State Alcoholic Beverage Control Enforcement Officers.

In addition to being trained for the duties directly related to the enforcement of laws regulating the manufacture, sale, and distribution of alcoholic beverages, the Alcoholic Beverage Control Agents, commonly referred to as ABC Officers, received much of the same training and were given the same powers of law enforcement as members of the Virginia Highway Patrol. Also, the automobiles the state provided for the ABC Officers were standard "police interceptors," cars that were equipped with all of the special performance and handling options that were found on the clearly marked cars used by the Virginia Highway Patrol. The ABC officers' vehicles were all painted plain black, with no external indication of the cars being law enforcement vehicles except for the extra-long, spring-mounted radio antennas that were standard for all law enforcement vehicles in those days. (For persons habitually on the lookout for law enforcement, however, that spring mounted antenna was often an obvious giveaway.) The ABC Officer's cars that my dad helped maintain in the 60's were Fords equipped with the well-known 390 cubic inch displacement Ford police interceptor engine. The cars were tricked out like regular Virginia State Trooper's cars, with twin 2-barrel carbs, heavy duty suspensions and brakes, and high capacity alternators and batteries, etc. In the context of his job, my dad was sometimes called upon to service and maintain the state-owned patrol car assigned to local ABC officer, A. B. Clements.

Agent Clements and my dad became good friends, as the officer would often wait around the shop and chat while my dad was servicing his car. Later on, Dad would sometimes tell me interesting stories about the status of moonshining in Patrick County, tales that he had gotten from his conversations with his friend, the agent. One of the things I remember especially well was what he told me when I asked about some people who lived near us and who, by all appearances, were engaged in a little bit of small-time moonshining. Dad told me that a mention of the individual had come up in conversation, and the ABC agent's response had been something on the order of, "Oh, we know all about him. He doesn't make much liquor and he hasn't poisoned anybody. We're too busy trying to get the big guys to worry about folks like him."

At one time, my dad said he had wondered if maybe the agents were being paid off by some of the moonshiners, but then he decided he was wrong to even think that. For one thing, Dad was sure that Agent Clements was totally incorruptible, and he also figured that most of the moonshiners he knew about didn't make enough profit to be able to pay off anyone. That was especially true moonshiners like the neighbor, someone who appeared to drink up most of what he made. Dad's opinion about the incorruptibility of his friend was reinforced when he overheard someone whom he suspected of being be involved with moonshining, spouting off about how he hated that "dadblamed revenooer" Clements. "A feller just can't make a deal with him," was the fellows complaint.

I had no idea who Agent Clements might be calling "the big guys" though, until I read about the big raid at Stone's Dairy in 1953. In that enforcement action, a combined force made up of Virginia ABC agents, State Troopers, and Officers from Patrick and Henry County Sheriffs' Offices converged on a dairy barn located near the Patrick and Henry County line. Inside the barn they found a huge illegal distillery of incredible sophistication that was literally operating underground, within a functioning dairy barn that was located near a busy highway intersection. The distillery, which actually was located underneath a false floor in the barn, was reported to have had a maximum production capacity of about a thousand gallons per week. Unlike smaller operations, the liquor produced by this still was not put in fruit jars or jerry cans for transporting, but was loaded into a milk tanker where it was stored before being transported to another location for distribution. The boilers were coke fired and the smoke ducted out through flues connected to one of the ventilators on the top of the barn. Legend has it that, although the still operated only at night, the location was revealed when one of the ventilators on the top of the barn became blackened by the smoke.

Clements would sometimes talk to Dad about getting him to "soup up" his patrol car, presumably so that he could chase down even more bootleggers and moonshiners. Now, my dad was a good mechanic when it came to diagnostics and basic repairs, and he could tune an engine so that it would run smoothly and efficiently, but he never had much experience in modifying engines to increase their power. Dad thought that it might even be unscrupulous for him to order the high performance engine parts required and install them on Clements's car while working on state time. All of Dad's objections were neutralized one day when the officer showed up at the shop with a complete high performance conversion kit, the pistons, rods, sleeves, cam shafts, and everything required to bore out a standard 390 cubic inch police interceptor engine to the equivalent of a 427 CID Daytona. Clements also had the work order from the head of the district office in Salem authorizing the conversion and a Ford manual that explained every detail about how the modifications should be performed.

Dad had rebuilt a lot of well-worn state truck engines, boring out the cylinders and inserting sleeves, replacing main bearings, replacing or reseating the valves, and all of that kind of thing, and this job was basically not that much different. In about a week Clements was driving a car with a State of Virginia version of a Ford Daytona 427 cubic inch displacement engine.

Clements may then have had about the hottest *Law Officer's car* in the county, but he sure didn't have the hottest car in the county, not by a long shot. Just as soon as Clements started bragging about the engine he had in his state car, some of the ol' boys that hauled moonshine started putting engines that had been built by L.O. Stanley or the Wood Brothers in their cars. The Ford engines built by those guys often won major stock car competitions, and although my dad was a good mechanic, he couldn't begin to compete with those professional stock car guys when it came to building high performance engines.

When Officer Clements would hang around the state shop and chat, he liked to talk about the adventures he had in his career of finding and shutting down the makers and sellers of illicit booze. Dad enjoyed hearing those tales, even when he thought they were exaggerated, and I am sure that it was mostly the milder tales that were passed along to me.

One of the things Dad told me about was how Alcoholic Beverage Control officers would often help each other out by working in each other's jurisdictions. The agents would swap locations from time to time, so they could conduct investigations in counties where they were not well known. According to Clements, one of the officers' most common methods of gaining leads on who might be making illicit hooch would be to actually set up a temporary residence in a new town. After hanging around town for a few days, they would begin asking around about where they could buy some hooch. Clements said that he found taxi drivers to be among the most knowledgeable folks when it came to who was selling illegal booze. No surprise there.

Dad thought that Clements might have been considered to be a rather handsome fellow by the ladies, and he looked quite a few years younger than his actual age. He was reported to have used that youthful appearance to his advantage in looking for likely sources of moonshine. Apparently, it was standard policy for an ABC agent who was new in a district to frequent the events such as the square dances and music performances that were regularly held at places like the VFW in Meadows of Dan or the old elementary school in Stella. They would try to get friendly with some of the girls there, with the idea of getting to know them well enough to be invited to their homes to meet their parents. Sometimes, the daddy of a girl the agent was investigating would offer the agent something to drink, and that drink would sometimes be moonshine. Offering someone a drink of moonshine was not a chargeable offense, but having been offered the drink was significant in that the agent now knew that the daddy merited further investigation.

One of my favorite stories about agent Clements was about the time the agent's seriously disabled patrol car was towed into the state shop where Dad worked. Dad had to replace the split oil pan, the bent crankshaft, all of the main bearings, and make several other, less serious repairs to the car. When the agent came to the shop to pick up his car, he was more than willing to tell Dad all about how that damage had occurred.

It seems that Clements had been driving on a back road near the Mayberry community when he pulled in behind an old four-wheel drive military surplus Dodge truck that was just slowly bumping along. The vehicle looked kind of suspicious to Agent Clements, mainly because of the bulky load in the bed that was all covered up with a tarp.

Clements bumped his siren and flashed his lights a couple of times, signaling the driver of the truck to pull over. The old truck slowed down as if it was going to pull off onto the side of the road, but then it suddenly veered off onto a narrow dirt path instead. The agent stayed right behind the truck, again flashing his lights and bumping his siren, but that had no apparent effect on the driver of the truck. The truck just kept bumping over the rocky and rutted trail, belching smoke and emitting a deafening roar all the while.

The path they were on was too narrow for the agent to pass the truck, and it had even gotten so narrow that the agent could not have turned his car around, should he have decided to give up the pursuit. Assuming that the dirt path they were on would either come out onto a better road or come to a place where both he and the driver of the truck would have to stop, the agent kept right on the rear bumper of the old 4x4, even as the road kept getting worse. At this point, Clements thought the rocky trail was going to beat his car to pieces, but then the old truck roared up over the top of a steep hill and Agent Clement was relieved to see that there was a cleared area in the woods ahead. Just before they reached the clearing, however, the truck straddled a big rock sticking up in the middle of the road. The truck drove right on over it, and kept on going.

Unfortunately for Clements, he was driving so close behind the truck that he did not see the rock in time to stop, so he just had to straddle it also. As he tried to drive on over the rock, the oil pan of the car's engine caught on the rock and split open. The car was stuck there, immobilized by the rock with the oil running out of the engine. As the Agent sat there in the middle of nowhere, with his car hung up on a rock, he could see the truck, just a few yards ahead of him, pull on through the cleared area and up to where the trail connected to another road. The truck then simply turned out onto that other road and drove away.

The agent realized that the car's engine was losing oil, so he shut it off before it seized. Unable to even attempt to drive his car off the rock, he could only radio for help and try to describe his location. It took the wrecker sent by the Sheriff's department a couple of hours to locate him, and they didn't find the old 4x4 for several days. Clements had the license number of the truck, of course, so the truck and its owner were eventually found.

The truck owner was charged with failure to stop for a law officer, but he claimed that his old truck was so noisy that he never heard the siren. He also claimed to have had no idea there was a law officer behind him and he couldn't see the flashing lights because the old truck didn't have a rear view mirror. The truck's owner ended up having to pay a $15 fine for driving a vehicle with improper equipment, the only charge for which the Commonwealth's Attorney thought there was sufficient evidence.

One of the things that Dad liked about Agent Clements was the way he could tell about an incident like that one and laugh about it. His was a job where, in spite of careful planning and preparation, things often didn't work out. If he was at fault in the failure, Clements would freely admit to it and just go on his way to the next challenge.

From what my dad was told, the system worked very differently than I had imagined, especially with respect to the way that most illegal liquor operations were discovered in the first place. He said that almost every time they found an illegal still, it was because of some kind of a tip they had received, information that someone provided for them, almost always anonymously. Often they would just be given vague information, such as there being an illegal still operating near some store or barn. Clements said that the ABC agents didn't spend their time skulking through the woods, randomly searching for illegal operations, like people seemed to think they did. That may have been the way the revenuers operated in cartoons and movies, but the

Virginia ABC Law Enforcement Agents usually went on specific searches, almost always after they had received a report or a complaint. He added that he thought that the most helpful information was usually provided by a jilted girlfriend or a business competitor.

Although Dad would sometimes ask the agent about someone he knew whom he thought might be a moonshiner or a bootlegger, Clements would rarely talk about any individuals by name. On a couple of occasions, he did reveal that he knew so and so was making and selling moonshine, but that the person's situation was one that deserved special consideration. "The ol' guy doesn't have a job and he's got all those kids to feed," he said about one individual. "He makes pretty good stuff, but he doesn't make a lot of it. Everybody benefits if we spend our time looking for the guy who is running a 500 gallon submarine still and is using a car radiator for the condenser." Clements said that whenever any dangerously bad liquor began showing up in the county, that was when all the stops were pulled out and all of the officers in the area went on the hunt.

All of what I am writing about here happened fifty or more years ago, and it has been years since I have read in the local paper about a raid on a liquor still in the my home county. So what has happened to all the moonshining? Has it all gone away? Well, my guess is that it may not quite be gone, but it sure has been effected by modern economic conditions. It has to be really hard for a small time independent entrepreneur to compete with a large scale commercial distillery, even if the small time independent has the advantage of not paying the current $13.50 per proof gallon in Federal excise tax. A quart of legal, drinkable quality, 80 proof vodka can be bought for about $20.00, of which $2.70 is Federal excise tax. Even if a moonshiner has the advantage of not paying that tax, I really don't see how he can make drinkable stuff and sell it for a large enough profit margin to justify the risk involved.

The last time anyone offered to sell me a jar of moonshine, which was more than ten years ago, he wanted $10.00 for a pint of the stuff, right in there with the price of cheap vodka. To the extent that any moonshining is still taking place in Mayberry, I only know of a couple of guys who are currently involved in making illegal booze, and that's because they make it strictly as a hobby. They don't sell any, they do their distilling strictly for themselves and their friends and for fun. The small quantities they make are either consumed by them or given away, and I suppose that there is little danger that revenuers are going to come busting into their homes and smash up the pressure cooker moonshine still sitting on the kitchen range. That is, unless law enforcement receives a complaint from an unhappy spouse or a nosey neighbor.

When I sell liquor, it's called bootlegging. When my patrons serve it from a silver tray over on Lakeshore Drive, it's called hospitality.

Al Capone

Some Mountain Dew for You

Lowlifes tossing trash into George's front yard had been a problem ever since he and his wife had moved to Mayberry. They grumbled about it a bit, but mostly they just accepted it as the price they had to pay for living in such a beautiful rural area and having such an inviting expanse of lawn. Their green carpet extended for over a hundred feet, all the way down from the front of their neat ranch-style home to the ditch at the edge of Squirrel Spur Road. "There just ain't no shortage of sorry people," George would say to his wife Gladys, as he would remove a beer can or a potato chip bag from the edge of the lawn.

George loved retirement. After almost thirty years of military service and twelve more spent working in a tedious job as a machinist for Nanometrics, all he wanted to do now was putter around the house and yard and maintain his little mountain estate. If you drove past their place any day that the weather was decent, you would likely see George and Gladys out working in the yard, both wearing their blue Dicky Coveralls. Gladys kept those coveralls so clean and pressed, the couple looked like they could have been NASA technicians.

Whenever someone would complement George on his

neat mountain place, he would always respond by saying, “Well, thanks. I reckon you know that if this place was in San Bernardino, it’d be worth more than a million dollars.” Gladys had heard George say it so many times that now she just rolled her eyes.

The assault on the estate began in an unremarkable way. As George strolled down his driveway to check the mailbox one afternoon, something on the lawn caught his eye. When he walked over to the Japanese maple, located between the tree and the highway and lying right there on his perfectly trimmed emerald green grass, he found an empty plastic 16 ounce Mountain Dew Light beverage bottle. As just another item among the variety of trash he would find deposited on his lawn, it was no real cause for concern at the time. But then a pattern began to emerge.

Finding the same kind of bottle on the lawn once in a while wouldn’t be anything remarkable, but when there would be one or two of them showing up on the lawn almost every Monday through Friday, week after week, every one of them found somewhere near the Japanese maple tree, the center piece of the lawn, it was not accidental. One morning there were three of them there! That was when George decided that there must be more than one bottle chucker and that he was being targeted!

“Them lowlifes got no respect for other peoples’ property,” George mumbled to himself one morning, as he picked up the empty drink bottle and continued across his lawn. On this day, however, he made a detour on his way back to the house. He did not chuck this bottle into the recycling bin, but instead, he took the top off and rinsed out the bottle under the hose bib. Then, once inside his immaculate garage, he dried the bottle off and carefully placed it upright at the left rear corner of his empty work bench. "George's work bench is cleaner'n my kitchen table," George's good friend and neighbor, Arnold, would sometimes observe."

When George went out to get the mail the next day, he discovered two more sixteen ounce Mountain Dew Light bottles on the lawn and they were in very nearly the same spot where he had found the one the day before. "Wouldn't make me so mad if they still had a deposit on them sumbitches," George observed, rinsing and placing the two recently delivered bottles onto his work bench in perfect alignment with the previous one.

Neighbor Arnold sauntered up the drive and into the garage one morning right after George had retrieved another of the bottles. As the bottle cap was screwed off, the air nearby was filled with a familiar aroma, one George instantly recognized from many years past. Along with the familiar Mountain Dew soft drink citrus aroma, he detected an aura of the real thing. "Damn," he reacted, "that smells just like mountain dew."

"Well, wadja expect it to smell like?" Arnold asked. "It's a Mountain Dew bottle."

"I'm not talking about that mountain dew" George responded. "This bottle smells like 'that good ole mountain dew.' You know, it smells kinda' like hooch… booze… white lightning. I think maybe the bottle chucker mixes good ole mountain dew in with his regular ole mountain dew." George took a couple more sniffs to confirm his analysis and then held the bottle up to Arnold, who took a quick sniff and nodded in agreement. "Either that or they're using lemon-orange-corn likker flavoring in Mountain Dew these days," he observed.

"Whoever they are, they must have a taste for shit," grumbled George one morning, as he opened another empty bottle that released an essence of both kinds of mountain dew. It also seemed really strange to him that all of the bottles being thrown into his yard had the tops screwed tightly back onto them. That did not deter him, however, as he would unfailingly remove each top and rinse out the bottle before replacing the top and taking the bottle inside for cataloging.

For the next month, someone would deliver one or two empty Mountain Dew Light bottles to nearly the same spot on his front lawn five days out of every week. "Well, I reckon at least the bottle chucker must have a job," friend Arnold observed, as he watched George number and date the most recently arrived beverage container with a Sharpie. Each of the empty bottles accumulated on George's workbench had been numbered in the sequence in which they had been found, marked with the date of their arrival, and carefully arranged in sequence. By now, the parade of bottles extended along the back of the workbench for half of its length.

"Why you doin' that to all them bottles, George?" Arnold inquired.

"Evidence," was George's terse reply, as he held the bottle up to the light and squinted thoughtfully. He was not quite sure himself how he might be able to use the bottle data, but he thought they might prove useful in the event of some future legal action.

George and Arnold, standing there by the workbench

discussing the possible legal consequences of littering someone's lawn, could have been brothers. They were about the same age, Arnold was a little taller than George, and they probably weighed in at about the same. But while the balding and slightly rotund George, usually dressed in his blue coveralls, looked as though he was ready for military inspection, Arnold, with an unruly shock of white hair, sometimes looked like he might wear and possibly sleep in the same plaid flannel shirt and denim jeans for several days at a time.

A part of the bond between George and Arnold was the extended time both of them had spent in military service. Once out, however, they had reacted to civilian life in opposite ways. George tried to emulate military organization in his everyday life in every way that he could, while Arnold was totally determined to leave all of that Mickey Mouse military spit and polish and everything according to schedule far behind.

George's wife, Gladys, had already decided that George was taking the bottle business a bit too seriously, and when she found out that he was washing them out and writing the number and date on every one of them, she decided he really had lost it. Any time she would tell George that she had found another one of those bottles on the lawn, he would adopt a grim expression and narrow his eyes, then holding out his open hand he would growl, "give it here." Then he would disappear into the garage to catalog and add the container to his collection. When George's work bench got almost full of Mountain Dew bottles, he put the first one hundred he had collected into a large plastic garbage bag, which he tagged as MDL 1-100, before stashing it in the storage shed out back. The one plus side to the soft drink bottle assault was that George, who had begun to pork up a bit since his retirement, was at least getting a little exercise as he patrolled from patrolling the yard several times a day, while looking for Mountain Dew bottles.

When Gladys shared her concern about her husband's obsession with the Mountain Dew bottles with Arnold, he told her he had already figured it out. "Well, you know what George's problem is, don't you? Have you ever heard of somebody being obsessive-compulsive? Well, if you'll just google *obsessive-compulsive* on the internet, a picture of ol' George will pop up." Gladys wasn't sure if Arnold was kidding or not, but since she hated computers, she never checked out Arnold's diagnosis.

"Well, I just can't stand the way the garage smells," Gladys complained to Arnold. "It smells like a combination of soda pop and likker." Or, as Arnold thought to himself, it smells like a mixture of *Mountain Dew* and mountain dew.

Ever since George had retired, the meticulous maintenance of the house and lawn had been George and Gladys's hobby. Well, for George, the lawn had actually become an obsession. The grass was always kept clipped at just the right height, the driveway was evenly bordered with variegated liriope, and the boxwoods surrounding the house were all trimmed and rounded. There was none of this white painted tree trunks or thrift covered embankments like folks used to have back in the sixties, though. "Neat and tasteful" was Gladys's mantra, and George followed her instructions to the letter.

At one point, George wondered why no one was throwing Mountain Dew Light soda bottles into Arnold's yard next door. The thought had even occurred to him that maybe Arnold was in cahoots with the bottle chuckers, but as he thought about it some more, he considered the fact that Arnold did not maintain his lawn very carefully. There could be soft drink bottles all over Arnold's yard much of the time, and no one would even know it. George felt a little ashamed for doubting his old friend when he realized that Arnold's yard simply did not make a very inviting target for the Mountain Dew bottle chuckers.

For the first few months after the bottles began to appear in their yard, George and Gladys were consoled by the thought that whoever was doing the tossing, the culprits would soon get tired of the prank and the problem would go away. For months they had been picking up that same kind of plastic drink bottle, even when the bottles were mixed in with fallen leaves or had to be pried loose from the frozen ground. So when spring weather finally arrived on the mountain and the assault continued, George decided that some more serious action must be taken.

Arnold looked over into his neighbor's yard one afternoon and could not believe what he was seeing. George was standing beside the road with a basket of Mountain Dew Light bottles next to him, and he was throwing them at the Japanese maple, one after the other. When Arnold walked over to see if his friend really had lost his mind, George paused to catch his breath. "I've got it figgered out!" he announced.

"Figgered what out?" asked Arnold.

"I know why the tops are on all them bottles. Watch." George threw a soda bottle in the direction of the maple tree, placing it just three or four feet from the trunk.

"Now watch this one," George commanded, as he screwed the top off the bottle before throwing it. The bottle wobbled and tumbled through the air before landing several feet farther to one side of the tree than the first one.

"Accuracy," hissed George. "Them sumbitches put the tops back on the bottles so they can throw 'em into my yard with greater accuracy."

Arnold really did think George had lost his mind at that point, especially after he tried throwing several of the bottles himself. He did not argue with George, but Arnold really could not tell much difference in the accuracy with which he could throw the bottles with the tops on them from the bottles without them.

In the months since the first few bottles had been delivered to his lawn, George had not thrown a single one of them away. He had religiously been numbering, dating, and storing them, and whenever Gladys would suggest that maybe they should dispose of some of those bottles, he would insist that they might be needed for evidence, should the culprits be apprehended and brought into the halls of justice.

As the drink bottle assault continued throughout the spring and into the summer, George decided to try a little detective work. He began asking around at the local stores to try and find out if the clerks had noticed someone purchasing Mountain Dew Lite in unusually large quantities. When he made such an inquiry to the young lady behind the counter at the Food Market, she responded with, "Honey, we don't pay no attention to what kind of drinks people buy. If they're buying a whole bunch at a time, they are probably getting them at Walmart anyway." George obtained similar responses from the clerks when he inquired at the Quick Stop and at Nester's General Store.

As an exasperated George vented his frustration to his friend and neighbor, Arnold came up with a new idea. "I'll tell you what I'd do if somebody was throwin' bottles into my yard," he told George. "I'd set up my critter cam and get a picture of the slob. As a matter of fact, I have a wildlife camera, and I'd be happy to help you use it."

Arnold went on to explain to George all about how he had bought an inexpensive wildlife camera a couple of years ago. He had used it only once, and that was to confirm something he already knew. He told George about the problem he had with some kind of critter getting into his garbage can and scattering garbage and trash all over his back yard. Just two days after he got the critter cam, his suspicion that a raccoon had learned how to pry the lid off of his garbage can had been confirmed. After that, he bought a garbage can with a critter proof lid, and the problem had been solved. He then put his wildlife camera up in the hall closet and had not taken it down since.

Of course, Arnold's wife had reminded him that he could have just gone out and bought a garbage can with a better fitting lid to start with, without having spent the hundred dollars for a critter cam, so Arnold was delighted to have an opportunity to put his critter camera into use once again. He brought it over to George's the next day.

As George attached the camera to the trunk of his Japanese maple with little bungee cords, Arnold provided detailed instructions about the proper aiming and setting up of the camera. The tree in George's yard where most of the bottles landed stood was about twenty-five feet from the edge of the highway. With the critter cam aimed from the tree toward the road, George and Arnold were sure that it would not be long before they would have a candid photograph of the nighttime bottle chuckers in action.

When George checked his critter cam the next morning, he found that it had recorded 112 blurry images of cars driving past his place at some time during the night. An occupant of one of those cars had obviously chucked a bottle into his yard, because the evidence was right there near the tree, but there was no way he could tell from the blurry greenish images provided by the critter cam which of the cars was occupied by the culprit who had done the dirty deed. George thought that he needed to take even more serious action.

George drove all the way to the big sporting goods store in Christiansburg, where he asked an outdoorsy looking clerk in the hunting and fishing department about the kind of wild life trophy camera that might serve his particular needs. It was really painful to have to spend the kind of money it took to buy the kind of camera that the clerk recommended, but since the guy seemed to know everything about that kind of technology, George took his advice. He returned home a few hours later almost three hundred dollars poorer, but now the proud owner of a real high definition critter cam, one that was guaranteed to have a much longer range and produce much higher resolution images than the bottom-of-the-line model he had borrowed from Arnold.

On the very first night after George and Arnold strapped George's new wildlife camera onto the Japanese maple tree, they got at least one picture of interest. Among the images of passing vehicles it recorded, one image was of what appeared to be an older model Chevrolet Cavalier with a blurry something sticking up above the top of the car. It looked like it could have been an arm extended above the right hand side of the car's roof. Also visible in the picture was a blurry image of what could well have been a drink bottle, caught in mid-flight between the car and the lawn. George thought the location of the 16 oz. bottle he found lying in his lawn that morning was consistent with the image recorded by his new wildlife camera. Not only that, but the photo of the Cavalier with the blur above the roof, the 86th image recorded that night, had a time stamp of 4:48 am. Now they had a time line on the culprit.

Corroborated suspicion, however, is not evidence. His new camera still could not produce a resolvable image of an occupant or a license plate number. Not only that, but all of the nighttime images were taken using infrared light, so George could not even determine the actual color of the suspected car. Even on his fancy new high priced critter cam, all of the pictures taken in the dark were displayed in shades of green. The new camera had, however, provided some useful information. Now that he knew when the assault had occurred, he could get up early and stake out the lawn. But how was he going to observe the culprit in the act when it was still dark? Arnold suggested that maybe George could lie in wait in his yard beside the road with a shotgun, and if a drink bottle came sailing into his yard while he was lying there, he could mark the car it came from with birdshot. That should make it easy to identify at some later date.

Aggravated as he was, George would not agree with that plan. While he was really pissed at the bottle chucker, he was not ready to shoot at him, not quite yet. Besides, if he shot at someone just driving by, it could be the wrong car, or there could even be someone in the car who would come driving back by and shoot at them. Anybody that goes around throwing Mountain Dew Lite bottles into people's yards is likely to armed, he figured.

Then Arnold had another suggestion. "George, maybe you could use a pair of them night vision goggles," he told him. "We used them in 'Nam, and you could see things with 'em just like it was daylight. Of course, everything you see through night vision goggles looks green too, just like the pictures made by my critter cam."

A desperate George made another trip to the Christiansburg sporting goods store, where he learned that night vision goggles are quite expensive. The same salesman who had sold him the critter cam, convinced George that any night vision binoculars he might buy for less than $600.00 just wouldn't be of any help to him, for whatever reason he needed them. It was an internal struggle, but George was a man on a quest, and he finally came home from the sporting goods store that day with a brand new $845.35 charge on his Master Card account. The salesman had also talked him into him buying a suit of camouflage coveralls, a camouflage cap, a camouflage ground cloth, and a camouflage high-intensity flashlight, all in addition to the night vision goggles.

When George came in with his new night vision binoculars and accessories and confessed to Gladys how much money he had spent, she was more than a little upset. After thinking about it though, she decided that maybe it was all worth it. It had been years since she had seen George as enthusiastic about anything as he was about catching the

Mountain Dew Lite bottle chucker, even if it had made him a little bit crazy. When friend Arnold found out all the stuff George had bought, he just wanted to know why he thought he needed camouflage equipment if he was going to be using that equipment in the dark.

"Well, maybe bottle chucker uses night vision goggles too," was George's logical response.

George's quest was delayed by rain for a couple of days, but as soon as the yard had dried out, he went to bed that night with his alarm set for 4:00 am. When the alarm went off, he rolled out of bed, went directly into the garage in his skivvies, and slipped into his new camouflage coveralls. Then he grabbed his camouflage ground cloth, his camouflage cap, his new night vision binoculars, his camouflage flashlight, and slipped out the back door. He crept around the corner of the house as if he was stalking wild game and crept down into the yard where, by the light of his new flashlight, he rolled the ground cloth out near the maple tree, strategically setting up his post just behind and to the left of it, There, he had a clear view of the road, but he would be nearly concealed from anyone looking up from the road toward his house. He got really excited when he powered up his night vision binoculars and found that he could see the road and the surrounding terrain with such clear detail.

The first few vehicles that drove past after George had established his observation post were obviously no one he needed to take any special note of, but then when one particular vehicle came slowly cruising by, George actually observed the culprit in action! Consistent with what he had seen in the critter cam photograph, as an old Chevrolet

Cavalier drove past his lawn, a long arm extended out from the right front window and swung up over the top of the car. The arm propelled a cylindrical object over the car and into the yard with such precision that it landed less than six feet from where George was dug in. Another bottle was backhanded out of the driver's open window at almost the same time as the first one, but it landed closer to the road.

George's suspicions were now vindicated, but major problems remained. He still could not read the number of the license plate on the vehicle, and he still could not precisely determine the car's color. On subsequent nights of surveillance, George observed several more projectiles of the same type being hurled into his yard, and at least twice more he had observed both the driver and the passenger hurling them into his yard. This was no accident! It was such a deliberate act that it even required that the vehicle slow down as it was being executed, but George was still unable to resolve the license plate number. All he could do was collect the Mountain Dew Lite bottles after the culprits had passed and add them to the collection.

Arnold finally offered up one more potential solution. "Well, George," Arnold told him, "at four o'clock tomorrow morning I'm gonna' be up in the back of your driveway waiting in my truck. When the chuckers drive by and throw out the bottle, you give me the signal. I'll roll down and pick you up and we'll get out on the road and tail them. We'll find out who they are and where they live. We'll track the rascals down." Why had they not thought of this before?

The next morning, everything played out precisely according to Arnold's plan. At about a twenty before five, the Chevrolet Cavalier eased by and a Mountain Dew bottle was chucked onto George's yard, just as they expected. When George signaled to Arnold with his flashlight, Arnold eased down the drive, paused to pick him up, and they hit the highway headed north on Squirrel Spur Road, hot on the tail of the bottle tossing culprits. Fearing that the car might turn off of the highway before they could catch up with it, Arnold drove like a crazy man until the taillights of the Cavalier came into view. Much to the surprise of the vigilante pair, the Cavalier did not turn off anywhere until it reached the main highway and turned east. When they caught up with the car as it started down the mountain towards the town of Stuart, it was with great satisfaction that George jotted down into his camouflage note pad, the make, the model, the color, and the tag number of the car. It was a late 1970's Chevrolet Cavalier with an amateur Aqua paint job and a Virginia License Plate number of ZEB 283. George commented as he wrote the license number down that he would probably remember that number until the day he died.

The vehicles were slowed by a large tractor-trailer that had geared down for the long steep grade down Lovers Leap Mountain, and they were forced to creep along down the mountain at about twenty-five miles per hour for the next four or five miles. Then, as they headed down the long straight section near the end of the trip down the mountain, the Cavalier accelerated around the big truck. Fearful that the culprits might realize that they were being tailed, Arnold hesitated for a moment, and in that time, a car coming up the mountain appeared and kept him from passing the truck for about half a minute. By the time they finally got around the tractor-trailer, the Cavalier was out of sight, but Arnold kept pushing. He just assumed that the culprits took the bypass around Stuart rather than the business route, even though he had no idea where they might be heading. The distinct tail lights of the Cavalier came into view again, just as Arnold and George completed the bypass and they caught up with the car as it slowed down for a traffic light. The Cavalier executed a right turn at the light, prompting Arnold to announce, "I do believe they are headed for Walmart." They were indeed. The culprits were going into the Walmart parking lot at 5:15 in the morning.

"Reckon they work at Walmart, or do you think they just go shoppin' at the crack of dawn?" George asked Arnold, as they followed the Cavalier across the lot from a distance.

"He's goin' shoppin'," observed Arnold. "See? He's parking right up next to the front door. Walmart employees have to park way over on the far side of the lot – way over there." Arnold pointed to the employee parking area of the store at the left of the lot.

"Well, should we wait out here or should we go in?" George wondered out loud.

"Let's just wait out here a while and see what develops," Arnold suggested. "Let's see how long they stay."

They did not have long to wait. In less than ten minutes, two scruffy looking characters, a rather tall young guy wearing a well-worn baseball cap backwards on his head, and a shorter older fellow with a beard and a greasy camouflage hunting cap emerged through the automatic front door of the Walmart. The taller one was pushing a shopping buggy, and the only thing George or Arnold could see in that buggy were several 12-packs of bottled drinks. They could not see for sure, but they both guessed they were all 16 oz. plastic bottles of Mountain Dew Lite.

“Shall we jump ‘em now, or shall we just tail ‘em?” wondered George.

“Jump ‘em? I don’t think we better jump em.” responded Arnold, “Them guys might be carrying guns or knives, and they’re younger than us to boot. Let’s just keep watchin’ ‘em and see what happens.”

The shorter and older one of the two Walmart shoppers pushed the cart around to the back of the Cavalier, opened the trunk, and then shoved the cartons of Mountain Dew Lite in next to what appeared to be a foam cooler amid a morass of other junk. Having completed his morning shopping, the older guy straightened up, turned away from the car, and pushed his hat back. He was directly facing Arnold’s truck when he lit up a cigarette, and from the combination of the morning sunrise, the parking lot lights, and the flame of the butane lighter, his face was well illuminated.

“I know that sucker,” whispered George. “That there’s Fletcher Holmsley. We used to work together at Nanometrics. And that’s his boy Delbert with him. I think they both work over at the pallet factory now. There ain’t no need to tail ’em no further.”

“Well, what are we gonna’ do?” asked Arnold. “I ain’t real big on confrontin’ ’em out here in the Walmart parkin’ lot. Should we go to the Sherriff’s Office and swear out a warrant or something?”

“A warrant for what?” sneered George. “Are we gonna’ try to get ’em arrested on charges of possession of too much soda pop?

As the Chevy Cavalier drove out of the parking lot, Arnold started to follow. “Hold it,” George instructed, his face contorted from the depth of his thoughts. “We ain’t gonna' do a damn thing right now. I have a plan. Pull up in front of the store and I'll be back in a minute."

When Arnold stopped in front, George jumped out and trotted into the Walmart. In five minutes he was back, carrying just one large plastic bag. "Epoxy," was all George said, hoisting the bag as he climbed back in. then he added, "Let's go to my house and get them bottles. I have a plan."

As they turned out of the Walmart parking lot and headed west on Highway 58, George started talking. "Now we know who they are, and where they work. Fletch and me used to be friends, but he never spoke to me again after he got fired. He was a half-assed machinist for sure, but I didn't have nothin' to do with his being let go. He got fired for nippin' at the sauce while he was at work. Can't nobody do precision machine tool work if they've had even a little bit to drink. I knew about it, but I never said a word to nobody at Nano. I didn't need to."

Then George added with a touch of regret, "I even knew Fletcher's daddy. He wasn't too bad of a feller, except that he drank way too much, just like his boy." George simply could not understand how Fletcher had gone so wrong.

George kept up the chatter all the way back to his house. Once there, George retrieved three large plastic garbage bags filled with bottles from his storage shed and then went into his garage and nearly filled up a fourth one. Arnold wasn't sure what George had in mind. All he knew was that he now had four 39-gallon garbage bags bulging with identical empty plastic bottles in the back of his truck.

"Now, let's go down to the pallet factory," George commanded, as they got back into Arnold's pickup. Arnold was still puzzled about what George had planned, and as he drove back out onto Squirrel Spur Road, he insisted that George tell him what he was going to do. Otherwise, Arnold told George, he could haul those bottles to the pallet factory himself.

George finally leveled with Arnold. "You know how long this has been goin' on?" he asked, answering the question before Arnold could respond. "Over a Damn year. You know how many Mountain Dew Lite bottles I've got?" George asked, and again answered himself. "Over four hundred. And do you know what I'm gonna do with 'em? I'm gonna' epoxy these bottles all over Fletcher's damn car. I'm gonna' make that ol' Cavalier of his look like a freakin' porky pine."

Arnold did not care for George's plan at all. "You can't glue bottles to somebody's car," He objected. "'Specially with epoxy glue!"

"Well now, you can just watch me," countered George. At that comment, Arnold slowed the truck and began to pull off onto the side of the road. "No sir! No sir-ee, no! You can't mess with a man's car like that," objected Arnold. "It may not be much of a fancy car, but gluin' bottles all over any car would ruin it."

"Well, he ruined my yard," claimed George. "He flung bottles all over it."

"Them bottles didn't ruin your yard. You didn't have no trouble pryin' them bottles out of your grass, and the grass didn't come out with the bottles neither. If you epoxy bottles to a car, it'll take the paint off everywhere one is stuck on it. I'd get really mad if somebody did that to my truck." Arnold's was the voice of reason, and he was finally getting through to George.

"Well shit, I reckon you are right," George conceded, "but now what am I gonna do with all these damn bottles?"

"Well, let's think about this," Arnold insisted. "Maybe we should drive on over to Fletcher's place. Do you know where lives?"

"Well, the last I knew, he was livin' at his daddy's old place up Haunted Branch. Fletch's wife left him years ago, but I think his boy Delbert still lives there with him. We'll have to go back towards Bell Spur to get there."

Arnold turned his truck around and they headed back past George's house and towards Bell Spur. Arnold was thinking real hard the whole time, but when George told him that he should turn right at the next mail box, he still hadn't figured out their response should be.

They turned off the paved road and onto a narrow rocky lane that wound through woods filled with dense undergrowth. They continued for what seemed like a mile before the lane came out into a cleared area. As they drove across the clearing, they found themselves looking across a sizeable pond and toward a long double-wide mobile home permanently positioned on the hillside just above it. "I guess Fletcher must still live here. That looks like Delbert's truck parked beside the house there," George announced.

Fletcher and Delbert appeared to be living beside the pond in a long double-wide that had a front porch running along its entire length. The home was positioned on a slight slope just a few feet from the edge of the pond and a few feet higher. A clear view across the pond was available from anywhere on the porch, and the fishing rods propped up beside the front door gave the impression that the occupants lived near that pond for a reason.

“When Fletcher was working at Nanometrics, he used to brag about all the fish he caught from his front porch, so I guess this is the place.” George told Arnold as they walked up to the structure. “He’d said he’d cast a float line out onto the pond from the front of his place and let it out as he walked back up and onto the porch. He said that all he had to do was just kick back on the old couch on the porch and wait for the fish to bite.”

Arnold was thinking about how, in the same way that George’s front lawn was so important to him, Fletcher’s front porch and fish pond probably provided him with his life’s greatest pleasures. “At first, I thought about us epoxying these bottles onto Fletcher’s front porch railing, but now I have a better idea,” Arnold told George. “How many of them bottles have tops on ‘em?”

“There’s a top on every single one of ‘em,” George responded. “Why?”

Later that evening, as Fletcher Holmsley drove up the lane to the front of his house, he was already looking forward to fixing himself a bottle of the concoction that was his own invention, a mixed drink that he had cleverly named “Dew and Dew.” Once he had one of those in his hand, he planned on just kicking back there on his front porch for a while and maybe casting a fishing line out into his pond. His anticipation was interrupted by his son.

“Hey Daddy, what’s all them things out there a’floatin’ around on the pond?”

Fletcher stomped the brakes of the car and squinted out the window. “Well dad-burn it Del,” he declared. “Hit looks like the pond’s plumb full of sody-pop bottles.”

Fletcher and Delbert both jumped out of the car and ran over to the side of the pond, where Delbert used a stick to drag one of the floating bottles over next to the bank. After he had retrieved it, he examined it carefully. “It’s a big-size Mountain Dew Lite bottle,” he observed.

“Dang it, just look at em’,” Fletcher noted, waving his arm at the bottles bobbing all over his pond. “They must be hunnerds of them bottles out there! And it looks like they’re all the same kind!”

“Well, where in the hell would anybody get that many dang bottles that’s all the same kind?” Delbert wondered aloud to his dad.

A Ho Lotta' Money

One of these days, I'm going to retire so I can spend all of the time I want in the Blue Ridge Mountains of Virginia. But for now, I just have to make do with leaving the city as soon as I can on Friday evenings, fighting the traffic for a couple of hours, and hopefully getting to the mountains about supper time. That means that I am likely to be stopping in at the Golf Course Restaurant, a pleasant place to dine that is near the Blue Ridge Parkway and just a few minutes from my mountain refuge.

Whenever I go into the Golf Course Restaurant late in the evening, instead of waiting for the hostess to ask me if I would like to be seated in the dining room, I just walk directly on into the more casual section of the restaurant called *The Grill*. There are a few tables and a long bar in there, and if any of my old friends are at the restaurant, that is where they are likely to be found.

When I stopped in at the restaurant on a Friday evening some time ago, the Grill was packed. Most of the guys in there appeared to be golfers, many of whom were loudly celebrating their great successes on the course that day. Unfortunately, I did not see one familiar face, and the only empty seat at the bar was between two rather large, middle-aged guys, both of whom I judged to be golfers who were above the median level on the inebriation scale.

As I approached the empty seat, I was considering placing an order-to-go, but when I got to the bar and asked if the seat was taken, one of the guys turned and pulled out the stool. "Have a seat, Buddy," he sociably told me.

As I hitched the seat up to the bar, the guy to my right shouted past me to the really big guy seated to my left, calling him "Bubba," and asking if he was going to have another one. "Well now, the name really fits," I remember thinking. I also remembered having briefly talked to them a couple of years before, when they had been there golfing with some other guys I knew. When I introduced myself and mentioned the guys we all knew, they remembered them as being pretty good golfers. They also said they remembered talking to me before, which I doubted.

As I tried to attract the bartender's attention, the big guy turned toward me as though he intended to chat.

"How'd it go out there today, Buddy?" he inquired, assuming I had just come in from a round of golf.

"Oh, I didn't play today. I just stopped in here to get something to eat."

"Well, I done great today," Bubba proudly volunteered. "Shot eighty-four, and that ain't half bad on this course."

For me, eighty-four is a good score on a par three course. "Is that eighty four net?" I asked. It's about the only golf-related question I know enough to ask.

"Yes sir! That's a net score of eighty-four." he assured me. "Eighty-four! And this here is one dang tough course."

The guy on my right, who had been listening in and had apparently played the round with Bubba earlier turned and joined the conversation. "Bubba there is lyin' to ya'. He got that eighty-four usin' his twelve handicap. He shot a ninety-six net." He then guffawed at his revelation.

"Dookie's the one doin' the lyin'," Bubba insisted,

pointing his finger at the guy on my right. "I'm down to an eight handicap at my club in Charleston, but today I was hot. I shot eighty-four net, on this damn course, and that ain't half bad." Bubba's voice got louder and louder, and he thumped the bar with his fist to emphasize his impressive score.

"Well I'd be happy with a ninety-six on this course," I allowed, trying to be diplomatic. The debate was heating up and the last place on earth I wanted to be was between two guys arguing over their golf scores. But, as I was scoping the room for another seat, Bubba calmed down and changed the subject. "Where you from?" he asked.

"I live in Charlotte most of the time," I explained. "But I come up here a lot. I have a place just a few miles on up the Blue Ridge Parkway."

Bubba continued to be focused on golf. "This course here is my favorite." he told me. "You play it much?"

"I've haven't played here in over ten years," I admitted.

"You kiddin' me. Well, it's one heckuva course. Me and Dookie and a bunch of other guys drive all the way up here from Charleston three or four times a summer just to play it. They's a million golf courses down around Charleston, but we like to get the weekend condo packages and come up here when it's real hot in the summer. It's umpteen degrees cooler up here in these mountains, you know? But to play this course anytime is worth the trip. You don't play here? Really? Where do you play? You play golf at Primland?"

"Actually, I don't play golf any more. I have knee problems, shoulder problems, all kinds of problems. It's been years since I played a round of golf." The knee and shoulder problems are real, and I saw no reason to add that I have neither the time nor the money to play golf, especially at Primland.

"You live up here, you must be retired," Bubba assumed.

"I'm not completely retired yet. I grew up near here and ended up with a piece of the family farm in Mayberry. Now my wife and I stay up here as much as we can, especially in the summer," I explained. "But I really don't mind staying in Charlotte in January,"

"What is it that you won't retire from?" Bubba asked.

"I've been in education mostly. Now that I'm winding down, I just teach."

"Huh. Teaching, huh." Bubba grunted in a way that conveyed a not-very-high opinion of teaching. Our conversation came to a brief halt, but failing to find anyone else to talk to, he soon turned back toward me and renewed the discussion.

"Teachers don't make much money do they?" Bubba was making a statement, not asking a question.

"You are right about that," I agreed. Then I leaned back, patted my belly, and added, "But as you can see, I haven't missed too many meals."

Our conversation was interrupted as the bartender slid a menu my way and asked if I wanted to order. Without even opening the menu, I ordered my usual, the grilled salmon Caesar salad and a draft beer.

"Gimme another one of these," Bubba ordered, shoving his glass across the bar to the bartender before he could turn away. The bartender obviously knew what Bubba was drinking, as he delivered what appeared to be scotch and water within a couple of minutes.

"Well, I waddent much good in school," Bubba confessed. "Teachers didn't like me. They didn't think I'd amount to nothin' much. But I showed 'em. I got my law degree and now I make a ho lotta' money. I make a ho lot more than school teachers do."

"I am sure you do," I agreed. "The cable guy makes more than teachers do."

Then Bubba leaned back and looked at me kind of sideways, as though he had suddenly become suspicious. "You ain't no English teacher are you?" Bubba asked, narrowing his gaze. "My worst subject was English."

"Oh heck no, not English. English was one of my hardest subjects. I am not an English teacher, my friend," I assured him.

Bubba appeared to relax, then grinned and began to reminisce about his school days. "I drove my English teachers nuts – couldn't write a correct sentence to save my ass. The only teacher I ever had that was worth a shit was Coach Williams. He taught history and coached football."

I declined to comment, so Bubba kept reminiscing. "Miz Purvis wouldn't believe it if she knew I was a lawyer an' makin' a ho buncha money doin' it." Then he added, "Mrs. Gaskins would go outta her gourd if she knew I was a lawyer. She always said that if I didn't learn spelling and grammar and how to write a correct sentence, I wouldn't never get a good job." Then Bubba raised his glass and ramped up the volume. "Now I got somebody does that grammar shit for me and I don't worry about the spellin'. I just count the money."

"Well, I don't worry about spelling either, thanks to Spellcheck." I told Bubba. He appeared to not know what I was talking about.

Dookie, the guy on my right had apparently been listening in on our conversation and decided to join back in. "You know what this guy really does?" Dookie asked, leaning across in front of me and sloshing his glass toward Bubba. "He screws honest corporations out of their hard-earned money."

Dookie then set his drink on the counter, leaned back, and pointed an accusing finger at Bubba. "Bubba's one'a them sleaze-bag lawyers like you see on TV. You know, the guy in the lawyer commercial that says, 'If you have been taking Spantran for erectile dysfunction, your dong may fall off. If this has happend to you, call this number.'"

I couldn't help but crack up at Dookie's version of the annoying lawyer commercial, but Bubba appeared to not be so amused. His face was red when he slid off his stool, walked around me and leaned over his nemesis. "Your problem is that your company specializes in making faulty products. That's why you're always getting your ass sued," he declared.

I was beginning to worry that this might escalate into a real fracas, but Ray, another member of their group reassured me. "Oh, those guys go at each other like this all the time," he told me. "Nothing to worry about."

"I do product liability and workplace injury litigation," Bubba explained, as he climbed back onto his stool. "It ain't rocket science, but it sure pays good."

Dookie had turned away and was reviewing his golf score with another golfer, so Bubba began talking to me again. "You teach high school?" he asked.

"Nope, I've taught in college for almost forty years."

"No kiddin'? What college?"

The bartender had apparently forgotten my order, so I waved him down as I explained to Bubba, "Well, my current job is with UNC-Charlotte."

"No kiddin'," Bubba grumbled. "UNC, huh. Well, what in the hell is the matter with them Tar Heels?"

I wasn't sure if Bubba was referring to game scores or academic scandals, but that was beside the point. "I teach at UNC-Charlotte, not the University at Chapel Hill. It's UNC-Chapel Hill that's the *Tar Heels*," I explained. "The UNC-Charlotte teams are called the *Forty-Niners*."

"No kiddin'. I didn't know there was a UNC at Charlotte." Bubba frowned. "What do you teach there?"

Our conversation was interrupted as my order was delivered, but without any utensils. "Physics," I responded, as I again tried to attract the attention of the bartender.

Bubba brightened considerably. "No kiddin'. What sport? Football?"

The bartender delivered a fork, so I ignored Bubba's question and concentrated on my food. Bubba shifted his banter to some of his fellow golfers and I dined in peace for a time. But eventually he again turned to me.

"What'd you say your name is?" Bubba asked.

"Most folks call me 'Mack'."

As the bartender removed my empty plate, Bubba held up his glass and ordered again. "Hey, get me and Coach Max here refills."

I assumed that Bubba thought he was bestowing an honor on me by calling me coach, as he again turned to me.

"What'd you say you coach?"

"I don't coach a sport. I teach physics."

That seemed to interest Bubba in at least one respect. "Don't teaching physics pay a ho lotta money?"

"About the same amount that teaching English pays," was my response.

That's a true statement, but Bubba responded with a totally irrelevant comment. "Ah, don't gimme that. They just hired a defensive coordinator at Georgia for almost a million dollars. That's a ho lotta' money."

"I'm not a coach, I'm a science teacher," I insisted. "Physics is a branch of science. Physics, you know, like in physics and chemistry and biology?"

About the time that the bartender brought our refills, the light appeared to dawn for Bubba. "Oh Yeah! Physics! Like lasers and space and stuff like that. Right?"

I figured that was as close as we were going to get, so I happily agreed. "Yep, physics: Lasers and space and stuff like that."

"Well, don't physics pay good?" Bubba asked.

Fortunately, Dookie reappeared just then, walking around to Bubba and thrusting a small scratch pad in front of him. "Speaking of pay, this is what you owe me and Ray on the round today. Time to pay up," he grinned, "or do you want to make it double or nothin' on the round tomorrow?"

As Bubba wobbled away from the bar, he and Dookie formed a huddle with some other guys. After some bickering, I saw several bills, some of them fifties, being transferred among the guys in the huddle. Looks like somebody is getting a ho lotta Bubba's money, I thought.

As the banter within the group continued, I finished my dinner, paid my bill, and moved to make my exit. I was almost past the huddle when Bubba reached out and grabbed my arm, pulling me over toward the group.

"Hey, you guys know Coach Max?" he asked his compatriots. "He's a Tar Heel. You ain't leavin' us are you, Max?"

"We've got a question we want to ask ya'," Dookie added. Naturally, I wondered what this was all about, so I joined the huddle.

"You from up here in these mountains," Bubba said to me. "Ain't that right?"

"Well, yeah, I grew up not far from here," I told them.

"So here's what we want to ask ya." Bubba was looking really serious as he directed the question to me. "Don't they make some real good moonshine up here in these mountains?"

"They sure used to make some of it around here," I told him, "but I don't think there's much moonshine being made around here anymore."

Bubba decided to go right to the crux of the matter. "Well, I was just telling these guys about how they make some really good moonshine up here. I just told 'em that I know a feller who's from up here and he could tell us where we could get us some of that real mountain dew. Now you ain't going to make a liar out of me, are you?"

I was thinking out loud as I responded to Bubba's question. "Well, let's see, the last time I actually bought any moonshine must have been more than ten years ago. I paid a friend of mine ten dollars for a pint and some other friends drank most of it. I didn't think it was that good. And that friend, unfortunately, is no longer around."

"Well, I promised these guys that I would get 'em some real ol' mountain dew while we were up here. Don't you have any idea where I can get some?" Bubba was obviously serious about his quest.

I had to think really hard about that. I probably haven't bought moonshine more than half a dozen times in my entire life, and I regretted it just about every time I did. But I did think of something that might help them. "Did you guys come in on the Blue Ridge Parkway?" I asked. They had come to the golf course via the Parkway.

"Well, on my way here, when I drove past the Pinnacle View Overlook – you know, one of those places where you can pull off the Parkway to look at the scenery – there was a guy sitting there at the overlook in an old green pickup." I then explained about how I see the guy there almost every Friday evening when I come up here. I figure he might be waiting there because he is selling moonshine… either selling moonshine or maybe something worse."

"Oh yeah! I saw that guy!" Bubba got real excited. "He was in a Courier that's been painted Earl Schieb green. I wondered why he was just sittin' at that overlook. Reckon he's still there?"

We had left Dookie way behind in the conversation. "What the hell is a Courier?" he wanted to know. "And who is Earl what's-his-name? Does he sell moonshine?"

"Don't worry about it," Bubba assured Dookie. "We just need to see if we can find a guy sitting all alone in a little bitty green Ford pickup at a romantic Parkway overlook. Let's go see if he's still there. It ain't that far from here. It won't take long."

I tried to temper Bubba's enthusiasm, telling him that I was only guessing that the guy might be selling moonshine and that he might be dealing in something worse. Or he might just like the view from there. But Bubba was determined.

"Be back in half a damn hour," he assured the group, as he and Dookie headed out the side door of the Grill.

Bubba and Dookie were gone for what seemed a lot longer than half an hour. The more I thought about it, the less confident I became that the guy really was waiting there to sell moonshine. I could imagine someone reacting violently to two guys coming up to him in the dark, so I hoped that nobody would still be there, waiting at the overlook in a green pickup.

As the hour grew late and the Grill began emptying out, I became very worried. But just as I was about to suggest to the golfing group that maybe we should go check on the moonshine seekers, Bubba's face appeared at the door. From the grin on his face, I immediately knew that not only had the search had gone well, but that the moonshine had already been well tested.

Bubba and Dookie shuttled up to the bar, each with a brown paper bag tucked under one arm. I guessed that the bags each contained a quart Mason jar of moonshine. Some places, there's no telling what the jars could have contained, but around here, if the guy told them that the jars contained moonshine, they most likely did.

"He even let us try some first," Bubba grinned. "It's the real thing and it's some real good stuff." Then he reached down into the bag he was carrying, pulled out a jar, then set it up on the bar.

When I told Bubba maybe that wasn't such a good idea, the bartender just grinned and shrugged. A little later, he showed back up at the bar with a tray of glasses and passed them around. "Anyone need chasers? He asked.

I asked Bubba what the bootlegger had charged him. "Not a ho' lotta' money," he told me. He said they had given the guy fifty dollars for the two quarts. A hundred dollars a gallon is about what I would have guessed for the price of moonshine these days.

The 'shine those guys had bought was barely drinkable in my opinion, but the golfers all outdid each other in exclaiming about what great stuff that genuine sure-enough mountain dew really was. As the evening progressed, however, some of the guys appeared to be diluting the liquor more and more with water or Seven-up. I thought that was probably a good thing.

As I slipped away from the group and headed toward the exit, I was hoping no one would notice that I was leaving. But as I headed out the door, Bubba called out to me, "See ya' Coach. Thanks a lot. You have a good 'un."

Thunder Road

Moonshining and stock car racing have long been connected in the minds of many people, mainly because it is generally known that sixty or seventy years ago, some of the top stock car drivers had honed their racing skills while hauling moonshine. Two of the better known drivers who were known to have done just that were Curtis Turner and Junior Johnson. There has apparently been no serious link between stock car racing and moonshining for many years now, but just as drivers such Turner and Johnson helped create the image of the intrepid mountain boys who drove fast cars as they transported moonshine, there were movies such as *Thunder Road* that helped to solidify it.

If you are old enough to have seen the awful 1958 movie *Thunder Road*, then you may already know how that movie helped create a popular image of the fearless Southern Appalachian Mountaineer who made his living by hauling moonshine whisky from the makers in the boondocks to the consumers in the cities. The movie also helped to reinforce the myth that every hollow in the mountains of Kentucky, North Carolina, Tennessee, and Virginia was the likely location of an illegal liquor still. *Thunder Road* and Robert Mitchum did about the same thing for the image of the Appalachian Mountain Region of the South that the 1959 television series, *The Untouchables* and Robert Stack, did for the image of Chicago.

When I was living in Boone, North Carolina during the late fifties, the movie *Thunder Road* seemed to play to a full house at the Appalachian Theater every other Friday night for about two years. I saw the movie more than once myself, but not because I thought it was that good. Watching Thunder Road at the theatre in Boone, was an especially entertaining experience because of the lively audience participation that often took place as particular scenes played in the movie.

There were always people in the theater audience who seemed to know a lot about cars, and who were stimulated to inject humorous comments into the movie dialogue. Many of those comments had to do with the magic Fords that were being used to haul moonshine in the movie. Early in the film, Robert Mitchum appears on the screen driving a 1950 Ford moonshine tanker, a car that morphed into a 1951 model at one point, then to a '49 model, and then back to a '50 model. In other parts of the movie, both Mitchum and some bad guys were shown driving 1957 Ford Fairlane 500's, cars that would transform into cheaper Ford Custom 300 models as they crashed. It was fun to sit in the theatre and listen to the car buffs in audience chant out the precise make and model of the cars as they would first appear on the screen as one model and then change into another.

It was also interesting how, obviously in the interest of product placement, the semi-bad guy revenuers who pursued the heroes transporting moonshine all drove Chevrolets or Chryslers instead of Fords. Some of those cars would sometimes even morph back and forth between those two different makes as they were being driven in wild chases over fearsome mountain roads.

Another factor that may have attracted the Boone audience to screenings of the Thunder Road movie was the appearance of some of the actors who also performed in *The Horn in the West. The Horn in the West* is a popular outdoor drama held in Boone each summer, and the guy who played Daniel Boone in that outdoor drama for several years also played a minor role as a mountain moonshiner in *Thunder* Road. There were allegedly other "Horn" actors who had cameo roles as mountain folk in the movie, so Boone residents who attended *Thunder Road* might have seen someone they personally knew on the silver screen.

Leaving the theatre following the film, it could sometimes be interesting to listen to the folks who had driven in from nearby mountain communities as they argued about just what stretch of highway was actually the original "thunder road," the real moonshine transportation artery on which the movie was supposed to have been based. The discussions one might hear while leaving the Appalachian Theatre could sound something like, "Well, y'all know that the original Thunder Road was 221 from West Jefferson to Independence, don't you?" Such a declaration might be followed by a disagreeing response such as, "No, no, no, the real Thunder Road was 167 from Jefferson to Mountain City! That statement might immediately be challenged with a declaration such as "It warn't no such'a thing. Thunder Road was Highway197 from Spruce Pine to Erwin." I even heard one movie goer make the claim that, "A feller who helped make the movie told me the original Thunder Road was 421 from Wilkesboro to Bristol, and that's where they filmed a lot of it too!"

I thought it inadvisable to get involved with any of the discussions about the location of the real Thunder Road, but those discussions did perk my interest enough that I decided to try and learn if there was a real thunder road and where it might have been located. I thought a good place to start would be with the ballad itself. The last verse of the movie theme actually provides an outline of the route taken by mountain boy "Lucas Doolin," on his final moonshine run.

> Roarin' out of Harlan, revving up his mill
> He shot the gap at Cumberland,
> And screamed by Maynardville.....
> Blazin' right through Knoxville, out on Kingston Pike
> Then right outside of Bearden, there they made the fatal strike.
> He left the road at ninety, that's all there is to say
> The Devil got the moonshine and the mountain boy that day.

Well, it's a long way to Harlan, as 'tis said in another moonshine ballad, and considering the routes that were available in 1958, it is most likely the mountain boy took US 421 out of Harlan. He would have crossed the Virginia line and gone through Pennington Gap and on to old US 58, since that was the road that shot the gap at Cumberland back then. After taking Hwy 58 through Cumberland Gap, he would probably have gotten on Rt. 32 at Tazewell (TN), and when he screamed by Maynardville, that would have been on Rt. 33. He could have taken 33 all the way to old US 11/70, also known as the Kingston Pike. The Kingston Pike was the major east/west route through Knoxville in those days, and Bearden was just to the west of Knoxville.

Somewhere near the intersection of the Pike and Papermill Road, the fatal strike was made, according to the legend. There is no record of a fatal crash occurring near that location in April of 1954 as the song says. In 1952, however, a car loaded with moonshine was involved in a fatal wreck near Bearden while being pursued by law enforcement.

Although Thunder Road may have never passed through that state, North Carolina fans of the movie can take solace in the fact that many of the driving scenes in the movie were filmed west of Ashville on North Carolina Route 19, between Weaverville and Bryson City, while some others were filmed on NC Rt. 9 near Lake Lure.

If one takes the movie (and the ballad) seriously, then there is always the question of why moonshine was being hauled over that route in the first place. If the moonshine was being made in Harlan, Kentucky, why was it being transported **through** instead of just **to** Knoxville? Was it to be hauled on to Chattanooga or Nashville, all the way across Tennessee, a state with plenty of moonshiners of its own?

I was spending some time in Mayberry, Virginia, during the time the Thunder Road movie was still quite popular, and while there, I happened to hear a cousin of mine and some of his cronies analyzing the part of the movie where a moonshine transporter releases an oil slick from pipes located under the rear bumper. The oil slick, of course, causes the pursuing revenuers to lose control of their car and wreck. One focus of the discussion was whether such features as the oil releasing pipes were ever really used on moonshine tankers. One of the participants added to the controversy by commenting that, although he wasn't sure about the oil pipes, he thought that some moonshine haulers had installed spark plugs in their car's exhaust pipes and connected them to the ignition system in such a way that the unburned fuel in the exhaust could be ignited. Not only would that cause flames to shoot out of the exhaust pipes, but some had also installed plumbing in the car that would introduce motor oil into the flaming exhaust. This innovation could produce a dense screen of black oil smoke that would foil any pursuer. After some discussion about how all that might be done, my cousin declared that it would be easy to install such a system on a car.

Well, some of the guys thought the cousin was right and others thought he wasn't, and the outcome of that discussion was an agreement that the only way to find out would be to install the required modifications on somebody's car. Since it was the cousin who said it would be easy, his friends pressured him until he agreed to conduct the experiment by installing a smoke screen generator on his dad's Chrysler.

The first stage was fairly simple. They mounted a spark plug in each of the two exhaust pipes, connected the plugs to an ignition coil, and then connected the coil to the car's battery through a switch mounted under the dashboard. The experiment was based on the presumption that enough unburned fuel passed from the engine and into the exhaust system that it could be ignited by a spark plug, and that proved to be correct. It was soon demonstrated that if you revved the car's engine and quickly let off the accelerator while flipping the sparkplug switch to "on," the exhaust would ignite. With the exhaust gases burning, the pipes of my Uncle's Chrysler became flame throwers that would project roaring tongues of fire for a distance of over six feet. My cousin found that with a little practice, he could cause flames to shoot out of the exhaust pipes of the car at will.

Stage one of the experiment was declared to be a success, but time ran out that day and the second stage, the installation of an oil reservoir and the associated plumbing and controls required to allow the system to function as a smoke screen generator had to be postponed, fortunately. Not so fortunately, my cousin and some of his buddies were at the Collinsville Drive-in Theater in the newly equipped flame-throwing Chrysler a few nights later, when they decided it would be fun to scorch the bumpers of some of the other cars at the drive-in as they passed by them on their way out. Someone at the drive-in, most likely a patron with little sense of humor, notified the authorities. The local police quickly responded and stopped the Chrysler just as it was exiting the drive-in. Everyone in the car was arrested and jailed for the night, but it was not until the hearing the next morning that they first learned about the seriousness of the offenses with which they were being charged.

The law that made a flaming exhaust pipe such a serious offense was not legislated in response to the movie "Thunder Road," they learned, and such laws were was not even limited to the State of Virginia, where this particular offence occurred. Unknown to my cousin and his partners in crime, those laws were created in response to the real-life fact that prohibition era gangsters were known to have installed flame throwers, smoke screen generators, oil slick dumpers, and all kinds of pursuit evading equipment on their bootleg liquor transporting vehicles. One result of the use of such devices, specifically designed to help the bootleggers evade law enforcement, was the passage of federal laws that specified draconian penalties for anyone found guilty of installing such equipment on an automobile, or of even driving or occupying a car so equipped. That morning, the occupants of the flame throwing car learned that bail for each of them would be one thousand dollars, and that if they were convicted, all would face a hefty fine, a suspension of driving privileges, and possibly even some jail time. And one more thing; the law also allowed for the confiscation of the offending vehicle. Perhaps the most serious problem for my cousin was that his dad, the owner of the car, was someone who did not take such hijinks lightly. Just like in the movies, the boys were allowed one phone call.

After an hour or two of enraged stomping around his house while declaring that those stupid kids could rot in jail for all he cared, my uncle relented and put up the bail for all of them. He even saw to it that when they came to trial, they were represented by a really good lawyer. This lawyer was able to convince the judge that the boys were just teenaged pranksters rather than hard core bootleggers, and that they had already learned an important lesson. The boys' attorney was able to get the charges against all but the driver reduced to where they were each assessed just a modest fine. My Uncle got to keep his car, but my cousin, who was driving the car, did have his license suspended for ninety days. That was okay, because the cousin sure wasn't going to be driving his dad's Chrysler anywhere for a while. Who would have thought that the authorities would have taken such an innocent prank so seriously?

Hot cars have been associated with moonshining since the beginning of prohibition, but has there really ever been a time when high powered hotrods transporting illegal whisky from manufacturer to market were running all over the mountain roads in the Southern Appalachians? Could it be that such activity was not as commonplace as many people would like to believe?

I have known several local fellows who may have been involved in a little moonshining or bootlegging and who also had cars with highly modified engines and beefed up suspensions. I always assumed those modifications were made with the idea that if the "revenooers" ever got after them, they would be able to outrun them and escape. I also was aware that the owners of those cars liked for folks in the community to believe that was exactly the reason why they drove those cars. The ownership of those high powered cars appeared to have had a lot to do with status. But it does seem to me that once Law Enforcement Agencies became fully equipped with reliable radio communications, the probability of any car transporting moonshine being able to make a clean getaway from a pursuing officer was greatly diminished.

In a lengthy process of looking through years of back issues of local newspapers, I was unable to find more than a few reports in which law enforcement attempted to stop a suspected moonshine transporter on the highway and when the suspect fled, the officers pursued, overtook, and successfully stopped and arrested the suspect. I also found zero reports in which suspected moonshine transporters successfully fled from law enforcement in a highway pursuit, but then, I don't suppose an official would have notified the media about an incident in which he pursued a suspected moonshine transporter but was outrun.

I did find several reports of incidents in which law officers attempted to stop a suspect who was driving an innocuous vehicle such as a Model-A Ford or an old flat-bed International truck. Upon being signaled by law enforcement that they should stop, the occupants sometimes bailed out of the vehicle while it was still moving and ran into the woods.

While a search of such a vehicle would sometimes turn up a load of untaxed whisky, the occupants would often have escaped being arrested. Officials would often find that the vehicle was registered to a fictitious individual, in which case, it would be confiscated and auctioned off by the state. The vehicles that were confiscated and auctioned were obviously being used by the bootleggers with the idea that, if they happened to be stopped and the vehicle confiscated, that would represent only a minor loss. Reading about occurrences such as these caused me to wonder about the wisdom of spending a lot of money on a high-powered, specialized car for transporting moonshine whisky, as opposed to using an essentially disposable vehicle for that purpose.

During the forties and early fifties, one of the cars most favored for the purpose of hauling moonshine was the 1940 Ford Coupe, and there were several reasons for its popularity. The car was a rather inexpensive vehicle to begin with, and it did not come equipped with a rear passenger seat. That made it especially easy to extend the trunk into the passenger compartment of the car and give it a large hauling capacity. The car's V8 engine also had a lot of power compared to most other cars of the day. The 221 cubic inch engine developed 85 horsepower in standard tune, and it was not at all hard to find a mechanic who could significantly increase the power of that flathead V-8. The standard engine had just a single down-draft carburetor and the compression ratio was only about 6:1. Adding two more carburetors and shaving the heads to increase the compression could easily result in an increase of thirty to forty horsepower. Of course, another option sometimes chosen was the installation of a large V-8 engine adapted from a luxury car. I knew of a couple of '40 Ford coupes that had big Cadillac engines installed in them.

For drivers who knew how to handle oversteer, the light rear-ended Ford coupe, when equipped with a stiff rear suspension and an engine with a lot of torque, was the ideal hotrod for high speed driving on crooked gravel roads. A few hundred pounds of additional weight placed over the rear axle was said to have made the handling characteristics of the car even better.

I have heard lots of stories about cars that were especially modified for bootleggers and which, in addition to the powerful engines and heavy duty suspensions, had tanks built into the trunk. Sometimes, especially in the case of the '40 Ford coupe, the tank could have been extended well into the passenger space and have had a capacity of a couple of hundred gallons. I have to wonder how many of the vehicles known as "tankers" were actually built though. I have to think that if the booze tank was not completely full, the sloshing of the liquid inside the tank as the car negotiated a curve at high speed would be likely to introduce some frightening handling problems. I did come across a newspaper story from the seventies in which bootlegger was attempting to transport a few hundred gallons of hooch using a waterbed placed on the floor of his van. Unfortunately, as the van was making a turn, the liquid shifted over to one side of the van, causing it to flip. Well, these guys can't all be rocket scientists.

Whether a bulk liquid is in a rigid tank or a flexible waterbed, I would think that there would be a number of logistical problems that would interfere with the efficient filling and emptying of a few hundred gallons of liquid from a tank located inside the trunk. If a tank is permanently built into a car, anyone could tell just by looking into the car trunk that it was designed to haul liquor. The presence of the tank would be an admission that the car was being used for bootlegging, and once used, if officers obtained a warrant and swabbed the interior of the tank, they would almost certainly be able to detect some moonshine residue. As inconvenient and fragile as the cases of glass canning jars used back in the day may have been, I have to think that they would have worked better than built-in tanks. Later, so-called Jerry cans, World War II vintage steel fuel cans which became available by the millions following the war, provided a good alternative to either built-in tanks or fruit jars. More recently, with the introduction of plastic jugs, the problem of how to securely and conveniently package liquid products for transportation has been forever solved.

The many stories I have read or heard regarding innovative ways of transporting bootlegged liquor have led me to believe that many of the more successful methods of transporting either bootleg bonded or illegal moonshine liquor were based more on the value of maintaining a low profile than the ability to outrun law officers. I found an interesting newspaper story about one such innovative bootleg transportation method from the sixties.

One Sunday evening in 1962, a car was pulled over by

a park ranger on the Blue Ridge Parkway in Virginia. The car, a 1953 Chevrolet Sedan, was occupied by three people, the man who was driving, his wife in the passenger's seat, and their young daughter, who was seated between them. Located underneath a blanket in the back seat, down on the rear floorboard, and completely filling the trunk of the vehicle, were cases of bonded liquor. In all, a total of 960 pint bottles of cheap, tax-paid liquor were found inside the car, all of which had been legally purchased in Washington, D.C. the day before. The only thing remarkable about the blue 6 cylinder Chevrolet Deluxe was the heavy duty overload springs added to the rear suspension to compensate for the thousand pound load of booze.

By all appearances, the occupants were just another family out for a Sunday drive on the Blue Ridge Parkway, but a ranger on the Skyline Drive up in Northern Virginia became suspicious when he kept seeing the same car with North Carolina license plates headed south almost every Sunday afternoon. The observation that prompted him to alert his fellow rangers farther down the Parkway, however, was that there were always three people sitting in the front seat of a four door automobile.

There was one guy I knew who really did have a superhot car, he really did put it to use for bootlegging, and he did outrun law officers on occasion. It was the most powerful non-competition car I had ever known about at the time. The car was a 1958 Ford custom 300 two door with a supercharged Lincoln engine that had been bored out to almost 450 cubic inches. But the car may never have been used to haul liquor the Blue Ridge Mountains.

The owner of that car joined the Army in the early sixties and ended up being stationed at Fort Sill, Oklahoma. Oklahoma was still a dry state at the time, so this guy had the car built so that when he would get a twenty-four hour pass, he could drive from Lawton, Oklahoma, to Juarez, Mexico. There, he would load up his car with cheap booze to haul back and sell in Oklahoma. He would take a different route each trip to avoid arousing the suspicion of the Highway Patrol, but even the shortest route between Juarez and Lawton was over 700 miles, most of it in Texas.

He found it necessary to outrun the Texas Highway Patrol on more than one occasion, and on his last bootlegging trip across the Lone Star State, the Texas Highway Patrol began chasing him using an airplane. The Patrol's little Cessna had a top speed of about 120 mi/hr, but his car could top 150. With those straight roads across Texas, the patrol could not keep him in sight, even from the air. He considered this outrunning of the Texas Highway Patrol as they pursued him with an airplane to have been one of his greatest lifetime achievements.

From what I have read about bootlegging in more recent years, it appears that transporting bootleg liquor in passenger cars was mostly for the small operator anyway. When the largest still ever found in Henry County was raided, besides confiscating the distillery equipment, the barn, the house, two cars, and a bunch of other stuff, the authorities also confiscated a milk tanker. The raid occurred as the tanker was in the process of being loaded, but it contained only about 800 gallons of moonshine at the time. I have the impression that many of the really large moonshining operations used some form of transporting vehicles other than passenger cars when it came time to move their product.

Another example of an alternative moonshine transportation vehicle was in the operation of what may have been the largest still ever operated in the vicinity of Meadows of Dan, Virginia. This moonshine operation was cleverly disguised as a landscaping business, and hardly anyone around knew that the business was just a front. Indeed, the operator did have rhododendrons and azaleas, etc. growing in neat rows in the field in front of his house. Often, he would be seen, driving his flatbed stake truck all loaded with shrubbery and tools and headed up Highway 58, presumably on the way to another landscaping job. The owner/operator of the business had been gone from the community for several years when an individual who had purchased the landscaper's house found that it had a large room built underground next to the basement. From the plumbing and heating systems in the hidden subterranean room, it was clear that there must have been an unusually large distillery operating in there for some time. A former employee of the business eventually told about how those truckloads of shrubbery that folks would see out on the highway were actually just bushes arranged around the perimeter of the bed of the truck, concealing the cases of moonshine in the middle. The landscaper got away with that ruse for many years, and he left the area years before the fact that he had been running an illegal distillery became known to most folks in the area.

Thanks to movies and television and the myths that some of the bootleggers themselves promoted, the mention of moonshining still conjures up visions of especially modified cars, loaded down with moonshine and careening over mountain roads with lawmen in hot pursuit for some folks. A few times in the history of Patrick County it did happened that a Deputy Sheriff or a State ABC Agent attempted to pull over a vehicle that was believed to be transporting illegal whisky and a high speed chase was the result, but it wasn't exactly a common occurrence.

During the time I have spent searching old newspapers for stories involving bootlegging and moonshining, I did read reports of a number of arrests of persons alleged to have been engaged in liquor law violations. Most of those reports either described raids on illegal distilleries that resulted in arrests, or covert operations in which those charged sold untaxed liquor to undercover agents.

There were a few unfortunate stories about events in which either a person who tried to flee from officers executing a raid on a still and was shot and injured or killed, or an officer who was involved in raiding a still was killed or injured. I even read two awful stories that described disturbing incidents in which moonshiners were charged with killing their neighbors because they thought that they had reported their operations to the authorities.

While there are a few famous stock car racers who openly discussed their involvement in moonshine hauling activities prior to their having achieved fame as drivers, there doubtlessly were many other, modestly successful stock car drivers who honed their early driving skills while hauling moonshine. For many of the small tracks in the Carolinas and Virginia sixty or seventy years ago, it probably was true that some of the drivers you would see racing at the track on Saturday night might have been transporting moonshine whisky during the week. Some of them may have even been using the same car to haul liquor during the week that they were driving on the track on a Saturday night.

One individual, a man who had been only somewhat successful in the pre-NASCAR dirt track racing circuit, turned out to have been even less successful with his involvement in the moonshining industry. He not only raced cars, but he built his own engines and set up his own cars for racing. At one time, the claim was made that he had one of the fastest cars known in the Virginia three-county region of Patrick, Franklin, and Henry. The vehicle was his own personal car, and while it was not for racing, it may well have been built with the intention of being used in the business of hauling moonshine. Unfortunately, he never got to really put it to the test.

The first that most folks knew for sure that the fellow was actually involved with moonshining was when the big operation described earlier in this article was raided. According to the newspapers, the racer/moonshiner had been working inside the barn that housed the still, but he happened to come outside and see the revenuers as they were closing in on the operation. He yelled to the others inside the barn that the law was coming, and then he took off running, headed for his car. The moonshiner may have been one of the fastest drivers around, but ABC Agent Clement, a former high school athlete, was a faster runner. The agent tackled the moonshiner from behind and brought him down just before he got to his car.

A few years later, the very same fellow was caught up in a raid on another large still, and again he sprinted toward his personal transportation. This time he made it to his car well ahead of law enforcement. He was apprehended at the site, however, because the carburetors on his highly modified and precisely tuned engine flooded and the car would not start.

The last I heard, the fellow had given up moonshining and was applying his mechanical skills to a less risky and more profitable business. He is said to have become more successful and better known for the race cars that he built for other drivers than he ever was as either a race car driver or a moonshine hauler. Happy is the man who can make a living from his hobby.

Down the Road Here From Me

The end of prohibition also put an end to the industrial scale manufacturing of illegal alcohol for the major markets located in large cities for the most part. However, many states and localities kept their own laws restricting the sale of alcohol for years following the national repeal of prohibition. That caused the localized production and distribution of illegal liquor to decline much more slowly in rural areas of the country such as the Southern Appalachians.

Beginning in the early 1900's, the use of automobiles and telephones obviously facilitated the distribution of illegal liquor from maker to market. But how was this distribution organized in the years before modern transportation and communications? And how was distribution being accomplished even a few decades later, when many of the people in regions such as the Blue Ridge Mountains of Virginia still did not have either telephones or automobiles?

As someone who was born in the Blue Ridge Mountains a few years before World War Two, I can remember when a lot of folks did not have telephones or automobiles. I also knew a few people who made and sold moonshine back then, and while some of them did have automobiles, almost none of them had telephones. These were all small-time moonshiners, folks who simply made a little moonshine for themselves, plus a little more to sell to friends and neighbors for some badly needed cash. They had to have communicated with their potential customers somehow.

Where I grew up, even if a moonshiner had owned a telephone, he would have had to have used coded phone messages to communicate with his customers. Our telephone service was a system of party lines with ten or twelve telephones per line. Half of the people on a line would pick up the receiver and listen in every time a telephone on the line would ring.

Before telephones, the initial contact between the sellers and the buyers of illegal booze obviously had to be made by word of mouth. Some of the folks who attended public gatherings such as church meetings and holiday celebrations used these gatherings as opportunities to promote and distribute their product.

I used to hear older relatives describe how contacts between sellers and potential buyers were sometimes made. My grandpa used to talk about how the Primitive Baptist Association meeting was used by some of the local makers as an opportunity to provide potential customers with samples of their moonshine. At those all-day meetings, events that usually included a potluck dinner set out in the church yard, many of the men would spend most of the day socializing outside of the church. The women and the teetotalers would spend the day inside, listening to one preacher after another, but even they were not too judgmental about the goings-on among those who remained outside the fold.

There would sometimes be individuals who circulated among those outside, providing any who were interested with a nip of their home-made hooch. If they liked what they sampled, arrangements could be made for a time and place at which a purchase could be made. I do think that it was rare for any liquor to be actually sold at a meeting, however.

There were some innovative and advanced methods of contact that came into use just after the war. We became aware of one on them in the middle of a quiet summer morning in the late forties, when a loud wailing sound suddenly filled the air around our house. The noise was something between the howl of an animal and the wail of a siren, and it seemed to come through from the woods on the far side of our cow pasture, somewhere from the general direction of Concord Primitive Baptist Church.

The noise lasted for such a short time that it was hard to locate, just a distant but loud, up and down wail that lasted for less than a minute. Suddenly, it would shut off and would be was gone. A few days later, it happened again, and after a few more days, we heard it for a third time.

One problem the strange howling noise caused for us was the way it would panic our cattle. The cows would come galloping across the field with their noses pointed skyward, their tails knotted up, and their eyes rolled back in their heads. They would come running up to the fence next to our house, run along the fence to the corner, and finally turn and go crashing into the woods.

At first, the noise had always occurred when Dad was away at work, but we told him all about it and described the behavior of the cows. His first reaction was that the noise was being made by a bull, and we had to convince him that no bull that ever lived made a noise like the one we were hearing. Dad was especially concerned because, anything that causes dairy cows to run excessively can have a negative impact on their milk production.

The next time I heard it the noise, I ran down through the woods to try and investigate, but by the time I got to the Concord Road, the sound was gone. There was a new-looking maroon Chevrolet coupe parked behind Concord Church, but I couldn't tell if it was connected to the noise. I was just a little kid, and I wasn't going go up to some stranger and ask if he was making that noise. Besides, I had heard of all kinds of things that went on behind that church.

A few days later, my dad happened to be at home and standing in the yard talking to his friend, Loy Harris, when the strange sound erupted. "What on earth do you think that is?" Dad asked.

"I can tell you exactly what that is," Mr. Harris responded. "It's one of those exhaust whistles. They are illegal in Virginia now, but some people have them on their cars anyway." Mr. Harris should have known, since he was a part time deputy sheriff for the county at the time. I told him that we had been hearing the noise once or twice a week for over a month, and I also told him about the maroon Chevy coupe I had seen at the church.

Mr. Harris said that he would see us in a little while, then he jumped into his car and quickly drove away. In just a few minutes he was back. "What happened?" asked Dad.

"Well, there sure was a maroon Chevy pulled in behind the church," Mr. Harris explained. "I simply told the gentleman in the car that everyone anywhere near Concord Church knows why he blows that infernal exhaust whistle, and that there have been lots of complaints. I also reminded him that exhaust whistles are illegal in Virginia. I don't think you'll be hearing that noise many more times." In fact, we never heard it again.

Later, I heard Mr. Harris tell Dad that the car belonged to someone whom he thought was probably a bootlegger. He said he figured the bootlegger was using the exhaust whistle to signal one of the moonshiners over on Light Ridge that he was ready to pick up a load.

In the summer a year or two later I was visiting Kenny, a neighbor friend, when his mother needed for him to go the post office. His family lived near the Concord Road, so the shortest way for us to walk to the Meadows of Dan Post Office was along that road.

As we walked, Kenny seemed to prefer walking along through the undergrowth beside the road rather than in the road. He would also keep kicking around trees and peering down into stumps and poking into bushes. As we neared Concord Spring, Kenny kicked into what appeared to be a pile of sticks and leaves, and then shouted “Hey! Look what I found.” Then he bent over and lifted a quart fruit jar up from the pile. The jar was about half full of a yellowish liquid, and Kenny, a year older and far more knowledgeable than me, pronounced it to be “moonshine.” I didn’t know anything about moonshine, so it just looked to me like maybe somebody had peed into a canning jar.

After a bit of a struggle, Kenny got the top off of the jar, and he then sniffed of the liquid. He declared that it really was moonshine, so I sniffed of it too. I had to agree, it sure smelled like I thought moonshine should smell.

Then Kenny, also more daring than me, declared that he was going to take a drink, and that is exactly what he did. After he was able to quit coughing, he said that it was some really good stuff and that I should take a drink. Even though he called me chicken, I declined. It still looked suspiciously like urine to me.

"I'm going to hide it over here," he whispered, as he walked into the woods a ways and placed the jar in some leaves behind a low brushy limb. We agreed that we had better not tell anyone about our discovery. We figured that someone would come back to retrieve the moonshine they had hidden, and they were going to be plenty mad when they found it was no longer there. I also thought that maybe Kenny knew that his older brother had hidden some moonshine somewhere on the Concord Road, and that was why he was searching along the side of the road in the first place. When I asked him about that, he claimed he knew a lot of folks who stashed moonshine along Concord Road, and this was not even the first jar he had found.

Through that and the next couple of summers, Kenny and I, often along with other friends, would walk along the Concord Road, usually either going to the store or to the Post Office. Kenny would always walk beside the road, kicking at the underbrush, checking out stumps, and looking for hollows in trees. I was with him one other time when he found some booze stashed beside the road, and he again sampled it before moving it to a new hiding place. This time he claimed that he was hiding it there for his older brother, but knowing Kenny, I'd bet that he retrieved it later and drank it all himself.

Moving the liquor worried me a little, and I sure didn't want to be around when somebody found that their likker was gone. I thought that there might be an unwritten code that one should never take booze that someone else had hidden. Kenny, on the other hand, thought that any likker hidden near the road was fair bounty for anyone who could find it. I insisted that there had to be some kind of gentleman's agreement about not taking someone's stashed liquor though. I had been told that local moonshiner Tom Jeff would hide liquor for his customers in a hollow stump near the Blue Ridge Parkway, and I never heard that he ever had a problem with somebody swiping it. But then, people may have been kind of scared of him.

I would hear occasional gossip about certain upstanding citizens of our community who would take a nip now and then, but who would keep their liquor hidden some place away from their home because their spouses or families objected to their drinking. I think maybe that was why Kenny was able to keep finding moonshine that had been hidden along Concord Road, and that reminds me of just one more tale.

One Memorial Day, way back when it was still called "Decoration Day," I was helping as my dad and some other people who were cleaning up the cemetery at the Meadows of Dan Baptist Church. I was working with a couple of adults at the very back of the cemetery near the boundary with the Blue Ridge Parkway land. There was always a lot of poison ivy and Virginia creeper that intruded into the cemetery back when it wasn't mowed so often.

As we were taking a break, a friend of my dad's casually commented, "Me and my brothers used to hide our likker here, back when we were all young and didn't have enough sense to not drink the stuff."

Someone must have looked skeptical, because the friend went on to tell all about how he and his two brothers were working away on a WPA project during the Depression. When the workers were allowed a furlough every other weekend, they would always come back for a short stay at their home, which was just down the road from the Church. He said they liked to drink a little liquor back then, but they were not allowed to drink it at the work camp.

They decided it would be nice if they could have a little liquor available whenever they came back home for a visit, so they made a deal with a moonshiner who ran a still over near Mabry Mill. They would pay for the liquor in advance, and he would have it conveniently hidden for them whenever they came back home. The first time they tried out their plan, the moonshiner hid the liquor in the woodshed at their house. The liquor was found by their mother, who threw it down the hole in the outhouse, so a better hiding place had to be found.

For over a hundred years, the most outstanding monument in the cemetery has been the bronze obelisk that marks the gravesites of William and Steptoe Langhorne, early founders of the Meadows of Dan Community. "Know where that moonshiner would hide our liquor?" we were asked. Of course, no one had any idea until he walked over to the Langhorne monument and tapped on one of flat panels mounted on each side of the obelisk. The panel gave out a hollow ring.

"He would hide it for us in this tombstone here," he told us. "It's hollow, and for a couple of years there, we always had a half gallon jar of moonshine hidden here inside this tombstone." He then walked to his pickup parked nearby and returned with a pair of pliers. "I don't want you fellers thinking that I'm kidding you," he said, as he began turning one of the decorative acorn nuts that secured the panel. The panel came off easily, revealing an empty space inside the monument. I recall thinking that it looked like there was enough space inside the monument to hold a gallon jug.

I guess a hollow tombstone would work just as well for hiding liquor as an old hollow tree, and it would sure be less obvious, although some might consider it disrespectful to the departed. Back in the days when moonshiners were selling their product in Bell Spur or Mayberry or Meadows of Dan, there were known to be hollow stumps or hollow trees where a buyer could leave some money and come back the next day and find a jar of liquor in its place. That has probably been one of the most widely used methods of distributing moonshine since the United States Government began taxing whisky in 1791. When somebody had a product to sell and someone who wanted to buy it, the commerce was bound to find a way. That first verse of the traditional song, *That Good Ole Mountain Dew* describes well how a lot of that commerce was likely to have taken place.

Down the road here from me
There's an old hollow tree
Where you lay down a dollar or two.
Then you go around the bend
And when you come back again
There's a jug of that good old mountain dew.

A Final Note: Most of these tales are fictionalized accounts of actual events, but many of the names have been changed, sometimes along with changes in the locations and sequences. Some who read these stories will have heard the original versions, however, and some may even know who the real characters actually were.

Before I began writing this collection, I thought that the folks who claimed that there never was much moonshine made in Mayberry and the nearby communities were probably right. In doing research for this book, however, I found that for the first half of the 1900's, there was more moonshine being made in the area than I had ever imagined.

As I began to write down these stories, I decided to jot down a list of the folks whose names would come up as having been associated with local moonshining in one way or another. So I now have this list of names of folks who lived in Mayberry and adjacent communities such as Bell Spur and Meadows of Dan, and who made, hauled, or drank moonshine. The list contains an amazing number of names of people that I knew, or of people I at least knew of. I was shocked, shocked, I tell you. But there is no need to worry, because I'll never reveal the names on that list to anyone.

ABOUT THE AUTHOR

Aaron McAlexander, a native of Patrick County, Virginia, is a retired physics and astronomy teacher. He now spends a lot of his time in Mayberry, Virginia, writing historical tales about life in these Blue Ridge Mountains.

Other collections of stories he has written include *The Last One Leaving Mayberry, So Much to Learn, This Old Store*, and *Greasy Bend.* If you prefer reading books about physics, he has written a couple of those as well.

For more information, contact the author at

jamcalex2@gmail.com.

Made in the USA
Middletown, DE
04 April 2023

28247614R00126